D0948337

CUBANS IN EXILE

GERMANS IN EXILE

CUBANS IN EXILE

Disaffection and the Revolution

by Richard R. Fagen, Richard A. Brody,
and Thomas J. O'Leary

1968
Stanford University Press
Stanford, California

F
319
· M b
F3

Preface

The study reported here is modest, both in scope and in intent. Working from aggregate data and from survey materials, we have attempted to shed some light on the Cuban refugees who entered the United States during the four years from the fall of Batista at the end of 1958 until the discontinuation of regularly scheduled air flights from Cuba to Miami during the missile crisis of October 1962. For a number of reasons, both personal and substantive, we did not try to gather attitudinal data on the second large-scale exodus of Cubans that began late in 1965 with the establishment of special flights from Cuba to Miami, an exodus that continues in full flow as of this writing. As is explained in more detail in Chapter Seven, we feel that the refugees who began to leave Cuba in 1965 are, in a very real sense, a product of the profound transformation of Cuban society that took place in the first four years of Castro's rule; for comparative purposes we have included yearly occupational profiles through 1967 on the second exodus. The first exodus, the phase concerning which we have data, was artificially arrested while at full flood, and by the time the second phase began it was not feasible for us to return to Miami for fieldwork to supplement what had been done in March 1963. Had we been able to return, however, we do not feel that our major conclusions would have been altered dramatically by whatever new data we might have gathered.

In designing the study and in analyzing and reporting the data, we have been guided by three considerations. First, we were centrally interested in who the refugees are and why they left Cuba. Except as postdeparture attitudes and activities are relevant to these central concerns, we have not sought to portray refugee life as now lived in the United States. We were interested in the causes of exile as those causes relate to and derive from the Cuban revolution. We were less interested in the consequences of exile, except as the exodus as a whole affects the conduct of Cuban politics. Second, with the exception of the final chapter, we have engaged in little speculation. Rather, we have chosen to let the data and the analyses speak for themselves. So much nonsense has been written about both the refugees and the revolution that we have considered it our place to ground our argument as fully as possible on empirical materials rather than on guesswork or wishful thinking. Finally, we have tried to present the data and the analyses as simply and clearly as possible. The study is methodologically neither complex nor innovative, and we have sought to keep our presentation unpretentious, while not violating accepted canons of social science scholarship. It is our hope that the reader primarily interested in the Cuban exiles will find this study informative, while those who are more methodologically oriented will find in the notes and appendixes sufficient evidence of the manner in which we have faced some of the difficulties involved in doing research on a highly mobile and impassioned population.

The debts we have incurred in designing and executing this study extend over more than five years. In methodological matters, Edwin Parker was particularly generous with advice and encouragement in the early stages, and William Paisley was equally helpful as the analysis of the data progressed. In both the wording of the questionnaire and its administration in Miami, the participation of Franklin Maiguashca was invaluable. The cooperation of the Cuban Refugee Emergency Center in Miami was essential; without its help we could not have gathered any systematic data at all. From our first contacts with the Center until the last, we received prompt and courteous assistance. During the winter and spring of 1963, when we were working with the Center, Marshall Wise, the Director, José I. Santiago, Chief of the Administrative Section, and Luis R. de Lasa, the Public Information Officer, were the persons with whom we dealt most directly. We wish to acknowledge not only their cooperation but also that of the entire staff. Every project, it seems, has a number of invaluable ladies. Ours were Sally Harms, who coded and tabulated most of the data, and Jeanne Friedman, who typed and retyped most of the manuscript. In the modern period at least, every project also has a patron or two. Ours were the Stanford Institute for Communication Research and the Stanford Studies in International Conflict and Integration. To Wilbur Schramm, Director of the Institute for Communication Research, and Robert North, Director of the Studies in International Conflict and Integration, we offer our thanks for supporting us both morally and materially. Finally, we wish to express our appreciation to all those Cubans in California, Miami, and Havana who took time to talk with us about the revolution, exile, and how their lives had been affected by the transformation of Cuban society. This is, in one sense, a book for all of them—for no matter on which side of the Florida Straits they now live, they are bound together by a common national heritage and the necessity of coming to grips in some fashion with the most far-reaching political event of contemporary Latin America: the Cuban Revolution.

R.R.F.
R.A.B.
T.J.O.

Contents

Tables and Figures

TABLES

FIGURES

CUBANS IN EXILE

I

Introduction

THE BACKGROUND OF THE STUDY

On December 29, 1962, President Kennedy stood before a throng of Cubans in the Orange Bowl in Miami and accepted in the name of the United States the flag carried at the Bay of Pigs by the 2506th Cuban Invasion Brigade. Speaking to the members of the Brigade—who had just returned from more than eighteen months in prison as an aftermath of the invasion—the President said:

Your small brigade is a tangible reaffirmation that the human desire for freedom and independence is essentially unconquerable. Your conduct and valor are proof that, although Castro and his fellow dictators may rule nations, they do not rule people; that they may imprison bodies, but they do not imprison spirits; that they may destroy the exercise of liberty, but they cannot eliminate the determination to be free.[1]

The President was followed to the microphone by Mrs. Kennedy, who spoke in Spanish: "It is an honor for me to be today with a group of the bravest men in the world. . . . I will make it my business to tell . . . [my son] the story of your courage as he grows up. It is my wish and my hope that some day he may be a man at least half as brave as the members of Brigade 2506."[2] Two days later the ceremony at the Orange Bowl was reported in an article in the official Cuban newspaper, *Revolución*. The article heaped scorn on the President and his wife, the members of Brigade 2506, and the exile community in general. The headline read, "Kennedy and Jacqueline Review Their Worms."[3]

For many years, discussion about the Cuban refugees* has continued in this manner and on this level. On the one hand are the Castroites, who do everything in their power to discredit the exiles. On the other hand are the exiles themselves, their friends, and supporters, who present refugee goals and behavior as just, noble, and unselfish. As might be expected, a casualty in this clash of views has been a proper understanding of the refugee community. Common sense tells us that idealists, opportunists, and scoundrels are probably all represented in fair number in the community, but even such a moderate judgment has been all but lost in the public dialogue.

This highly charged dialogue—fanned by the continuing confrontation between Castro and the United States—has left almost no residue of knowledge about the exiles as individuals. Little is known about who the exiles are, their social characteristics, why they left, what they believe, or their hopes, fears, and aspirations. It is our contention that the wrong questions have been asked, that the "worms or heroes" polemic usually tells us more about the discussants than about the exiles. It is our hope that in the chapters that follow we have asked some of the right questions and that our answers will supply the bases of understanding upon which a more measured and enduring evaluation of the exile community can be built.

It would be misleading, however, to suggest that our interest

* Throughout this book we will use the terms "exile" and "refugee" interchangeably to relieve the tedium of exclusive dependence upon one or the other expression. Exile, with its political connotations and sense of "wanting to return," is perhaps the more accurate descriptive term.

in the Cuban exiles stems solely from a desire to increase public understanding of their personal histories and attitudes. In addition, we were drawn to this study by problems of more general significance. First, we saw in the Cuban experience an opportunity to examine in some detail the wellsprings of individual political behavior. Almost everything we know about political behavior tells us that normally the vast majority of citizens in all nations are politically unconcerned, unaware, and inactive. They do not think much about politics, they do not talk much about politics, and unless forced to, a large minority (and sometimes a majority) do not even vote.[4]

How does this image of politically inactive man square with the facts of exile? Do only the highly politicized flee? Is the Cuban refugee community composed primarily of political activists—on the one hand ex-followers of Batista fleeing from revolutionary justice, and on the other hand sturdy lovers of liberty fleeing from revolutionary tyranny? Is there something about a revolution that turns normally apathetic citizens into politically conscious and concerned individuals? If we accept at the outset the notion that Castro's rule was not "politics as usual" for Cuba, then we are led naturally to an examination of the way the revolutionary situation affected individual lives. In so doing, however, we leave open the question of how "political" the refugees are. Although Castro's rule is not politics as usual, we must not automatically assume that every exile is therefore a politically active and informed individual.

Second, we saw in the Cuban experience an opportunity to examine the conditions under which a political system generates sufficient internal dissatisfaction to lead to a significant exodus of citizens. This is a corollary of our concern with individual behavior. If first we asked how citizens must be touched by the revolution before they seek exile, now we ask what activities and programs of the regime were most directly responsible for the exodus. The answer to the second question is not the same as the answer to the first, for we must not assume that the new rulers of Cuba set for themselves the goal of driving out the majority of those who are now in exile. Rather, it is safer to assume that they intended to transform the social and political order radically, and that as a partially unintended consequence they brought pressures to bear on citizens in many walks of life. The explanation of the political origins of these pressures is not the same as the explanation of the manner in which the revolution was perceived and experienced by those who were caught up in the processes of change.

It should be clear from what has been said to this point that we do not view the influx of Cubans into the United States as just another wave in the flood of immigrants who have entered since colonial times.[5] Rather, without attempting to prejudge the issue, we have chosen to think of the Cuban exodus as a case of *self-imposed political exile*, which may or may not have important antecedents in the American experience. By this we mean that a preliminary overview of the Cuban situation has led us to select two characteristics that serve to differentiate it from other types of population movements, both into the United States and in other parts of the world.

First, the conditions that prevailed in Cuba at the time of the exodus were, in the fullest sense of the word, *revolutionary*. A massive restructuring of the social and political order by the Castro government was under way, and millions of lives were being transformed or at least profoundly affected by government action. The transformation was under the direction of an elite possessed of great power and committed to radical change. Even though the refugees themselves may not have viewed their decision to leave as directly related to politics, we feel justified in speaking of their exile as *political*, in the sense that the Cuban revolution was the "first cause" of the outflow, no matter in what guise the revolution touched the lives of individuals. Thus, we wish to differentiate the Cuban case from essentially nonpolitical migrations, such as the Puerto Rican.*

* In a case study of the motivations behind Puerto Ricans' decisions to emigrate to the United States, C. Wright Mills, Clarence Senior, and Rose

Second, the exile was *self-imposed.* Over the past decade, Berlin, Hong Kong, Vienna, and Miami have all at times become the focal points of international attention, as German, Chinese, Hungarian, and Cuban refugees have fled from the regimes in power in their native lands. To the social scientist and citizen concerned with the relationship of rulers to the ruled, this international flow of refugees is of special interest, for in the majority of cases these refugees did not flee for their lives, nor were they displaced either by the physical destruction of their homeland or by the reallocation of national territory.

We are dealing with a phenomenon that seems to differ from such exoduses as those of the Jews from Germany in the late 1930's (in which a religious minority was singled out for extreme persecution), the Arabs from Palestine in the late 1940's (in which a national group was dislocated by the creation of the State of Israel and the ensuing Arab-Israeli War), or the Moslems from India in the late 1940's (in which partition left part of a religious community alone in hostile territory). The East German, Chinese, Hungarian, and Cuban refugees do not constitute a religious or ethnic subgroup set apart from the majority of their fellow countrymen, and they generally did not flee under the threat of massive and imminent persecution, destruc-

---

Goldsen have utilized the "push-pull" concept. They found that the great majority of those who came to the U.S. mainland were "pulled" by hopes of economic betterment rather than "pushed" by intolerable living or political conditions in Puerto Rico (*The Puerto Rican Journey* [New York, 1950]). We do not mean to suggest that those who are pushed out of one system as a consequence of political upheaval may not be drawn to another system by expectations of economic opportunity. That Cubans and others have gone to the United States rather than to Uruguay or even Canada is explained by several factors, not the least of which is the "land of opportunity" reputation the U.S. enjoys. One case in United States history that may be similar to the Cuban is that of the immigration of German refugees into this country after the Revolution of 1848. Not all of these refugees were deeply concerned with political issues, but there is no question that without the political tensions, disruptions, and turmoil of those years in Germany, most never would have left the continent (see Carl F. Wittke, *Refugees of Revolution* [Philadelphia, 1952] and Marcus Lee Hansen, "The Revolutions of 1848 and German Emigration," *Journal of Economics and Business History*, II, 4 [August 1930], 630–58).

tion, or physical dislocation. Rather, their refugee status derives from some complex of personal experiences that they came to perceive as intolerable. What constitutes an "intolerable" set of personal experiences differs greatly among individuals, and because the self-imposed exiles are not meaningfully typed in terms of religion, ethnic background, or even political beliefs, neither the motivational nor the sociological characteristics of the refugees are immediately apparent. That is, without detailed research we cannot understand the Cuban exile flow in the same way that we "understand" the outflow of Jews from Germany in the 1930's, given the policies of Hitler, or the exodus of Moslems from India.[6]

The postwar instances of self-imposed political exile have stemmed primarily from popular dissatisfaction with governments in Hungary, in East Germany, in China, and to a lesser extent in the Soviet Union and Eastern Europe. All of these cases involved political developments that are in part parallel to developments in Castro's Cuba, i.e., revolutionary or at least new governments came to be considered unacceptable by certain sectors of the population. Despite significant variations in the details of these exile movements, the similarities are sufficient to warrant comparison.

Unfortunately, the available literature on self-imposed political exile is meager and of uneven quality. Very few systematic assessments of the several exile populations have been made. With respect to the flight of East Germans to the West, for example, there is little information aside from that distributed by the German Federal Republic. Similarly, very little work has been done on the Chinese who have fled to Hong Kong from the mainland. Only the exile movements originating in Russia and Hungary have been subjected to any extensive analysis.[7]

Despite these writings on the Chinese, Russian, and Hungarian emigrés, and the discussions of migration and disaffection in the general literature on political behavior, we have found it difficult to put our study in a comparative or theoretical con-

text. The atypical variety of behavior with which we are dealing—the decision to leave one's native land in the wake of a
far-reaching revolution—has not been given high priority in
research; therefore we approach our subject with some caution.
We hope to contribute not only to an understanding of the
refugees themselves, but also (in a preliminary way) to an
understanding of the conditions under which extreme political
alienation occurs. Cuba, in common with many other countries
in the postwar world, has undergone an acute crisis of legitimacy. Such crises are a result of the combined and common
experiences of many individuals. These experiences are derived
from and conditioned by changes in the national system. Thus,
throughout the chapters that follow, we shall concentrate both
on the refugees as actors and on the revolution that thrust them
into exile. It is not possible to understand the one without the
other.

Before describing our method of research, we must bring
the primary subject of our investigation into sharper focus.
Simply stated, we are interested in explaining *why* the refugees
left Cuba. The decision to leave is at the heart of our study.
Self-imposed exile is not a "little" decision, in the sense that
voting or not voting in this or that bond election is—from the
point of view of the individual—a little decision. The ties that
bind a citizen to his country are ordinarily both complex and
strong. And even when the sense of national identity is not well-
developed, inertia, fear, ignorance, and lack of resources usually
combine to keep a citizen at home. Perceptive observers have
noted again and again that individuals seek to satisfy their
basic needs in the cultural context into which they are social-
ized.[8] Only when this context fails the individual in some fundamental fashion does he begin to consider exile as a possible
alternative to continuing on as usual. Even then, despite indi-
cations that the familiar cultural fabric is coming apart at the
seams, many individuals remain reluctant to leave the society
and culture of which they still feel a part. Consider, for example,

the fact that despite a palpable increase in personal danger, most German Jews did not flee in the 1930's. While the explanation of this reluctance to leave Germany is complex, at least part lies in the perception by many Jews that Germany, with all its short-comings, was *home*—the only conceivable place to live.

Reinforcing the positive factors that tie an individual to his homeland are other factors that constrain his movement. Politi-cal and economic barriers to travel are important in many in-stances, as are the problems of language and work that usually face migrants to a new land. Leaving one's cultural context means more than trading familiarity for novelty; it often means painful readjustment in one's style of life and self-perceptions. Leaving one's state, by and large, means leaving one's status,* thereby undercutting the social bases for personal security and feelings of worth.[9] We do not mean to assert that the decision to leave Cuba was in all cases an act of moral importance or individual heroism. According to certain values or under cer-tain circumstances it may well have been that; according to other values or under other circumstances it was not. However we may evaluate it, we assume in most cases that it was not easily made, and we feel that in the aggregate the decisions are not easily or obviously explained.

Our search for an explanation of the decision to go into exile has led us to examine several types of factors. Taking some cues from the literature on political refugees, we have looked at the demographic characteristics of the exile community, attitudinal factors such as feelings toward the past and present regimes, participation factors such as degree of involvement in revolu-tionary and counterrevolutionary activities, and salient experi-

---

* For some of the downtrodden, leaving one's homeland may result in a relative improvement in life-style. But for many others, the move results in lowered status. Generally speaking, migrants usually end up at the bottom of the social ladder. Whether this lowest rung is an improvement over their prior status obviously depends on the conditions from which they came (see Bernard Berelson and Gary Steiner, *Human Behavior* [New York, 1964], pp. 466–67).

ences under the revolutionary government that relate to the decision to leave. Similar factors, taken singly and in combination, have been used to explain the departure decisions made by exiles during the American, Russian, Chinese, and Hungarian revolutions.[10] Thus we have used the literature on political exile as a source of possibly relevant variables, but not as a source of hypotheses.

THE CONDUCT OF THE RESEARCH

Our research design, in common with all others, represents a series of decisions and compromises that affects our analyses and conclusions. Hence it seems desirable to incorporate into the first chapter a sketch of our procedures.

The planning phase of this study dates from early in the fall of 1962, when a colleague of ours was in Miami. Curious about the exile community, he talked to a number of refugees. His informal interviews with exile leaders, recent arrivals, and long-established residents suggested that the community was in several respects extremely heterogeneous. Not only—as was widely known—were there deep political and ideological cleavages among the exiles, but there also seemed to be a wide variety of social and economic types. Somewhat surprisingly, political indifference and disengagement were fairly widespread.

Our interest was quickened by these impressions of the exiles, and we discussed the possibility of conducting some systematic research on the community. Several aspects of the Miami situation made such a study feasible. First, the exiles were concentrated in and around the city, making the logistics of research fairly simple. Second, through our colleague's visit we had established contacts in the community, and these individuals seemed anxious to help in any way possible. Third, in the Cuban Refugee Emergency Center in Miami there existed a potential institutional base for a field study.[11] We had three problems, however: lack of free time, lack of money, and the distance from

California to Miami. The effect these had upon our research design and procedures will become apparent.

In the early stages of drawing up a research design, it became obvious that we would have to enlist the full cooperation of the Cuban Refugee Center. We wanted to gather data on a sample of exiles who were in some way representative of the larger community, and the only list from which such a sample could be drawn was held in the records of the Center. These records, however, were not open to the public.[12] No amount of correspondence or proof of security clearance ever succeeded in gaining for us personal access to the main Center files. Fortunately, once we had convinced the Center's administrative personnel of our seriousness, they cooperated with us wholeheartedly, drawing our sample, doing secretarial work, and helping in every way possible to expedite our research while maintaining the security of their files.

Our original research design was based on the supposition that we might be able to find enough time and money to go to Miami and interview about 100 exiles. We hoped that the Refugee Center would draw a sample of 100 names and addresses according to our specifications and turn this list over to us, after which we would proceed independently with the interviews. Soon, however, two defects in this plan became apparent. First, for a variety of good reasons the administrative staff of the Center would not turn over a list of exile names and addresses to two professors about whom they knew little and whom they had never met. Second, with a sample of only 100 individuals we would not be able to do the types of subanalyses we were planning. We needed a larger sample, but saw no way of financing a more extensive interview design. A compromise of some sort was called for. Thus we began thinking seriously about using self-administered questionnaires instead of interviews. We were encouraged by the experience of members of the Harvard University Russian Research Center, who found that in their work with Russian refugees a self-administered questionnaire was very nearly as effective as a more costly, time-consuming, and difficult-to-administer interview.[13]

Our decision to switch to a self-administered questionnaire was reinforced by an experience we had on Washington's Birthday. A group of Cuban exiles in the San Francisco area had arranged a gathering to publicly pay their respects to the "Father of [their] adopted country." We arranged to attend the gathering in order to meet and talk with local exile leaders. During the discussions that followed, it became apparent that only the most fluent, skillful, and highly trained interviewer could hope to maintain control over an interview with an articulate and voluble refugee. The passion with which the exiles spoke about political matters in general and their homeland in particular, and the great amount of historical and political allusion woven into their discourse, militated against a highly structured interview situation. We realized that given our limited resources, even our original estimate of 100 interviews in Miami was optimistic.

Once we had designed a questionnaire, we arranged to gather a group of exiles of varying social and economic backgrounds in San Francisco in order to give it a preliminary test. After administering the pretest to this group, we discussed both the questionnaire and the general political situation in Cuba. Although this session provided neither the heterogeneity of background nor the number of exiles that we had hoped for, it did enable us to discover and correct some serious weaknesses in the questionnaire. (The final questionnaire is reproduced in English and in Spanish in Appendix A.) We then developed our final research plan.

The Refugee Center had an IBM card file (arranged alphabetically by last name) of the approximately 160,000 Cuban men, women, and children who had registered with the Center since it had opened. The Center administrative staff agreed to take a one-in-400 sample (every 400th name) from that file and determine the addresses, occupations, and ages of the selected individuals. We specified that the *final* sample was to include only male heads of households currently living in the Miami area.* If the name on a card selected initially was that of a woman, child, non-head of household, or relocated exile, the staff was to select the next card, continuing this process until coming to an individual who met all of our requirements. Using this procedure the Center staff assembled a list of 401 names and gave each a code number. These 401 Cuban exiles constituted our final sample.

Each member of the final sample was sent a letter inviting him to come to the Center on any one of four designated evenings. The letter explained that the recipient had been selected to be a member of a group that would be interviewed about personal experiences in Cuba. (The text of this letter is reproduced in Appendix A.) The recipient was instructed to bring the letter to the Center. Each letter carried a code number corresponding to the number assigned to the exile when the sample was drawn, enabling us to identify those who came and those who did not. One dollar to cover travel expenses to and from the Center was promised. Four days later each member of the sample was sent a reminder, to which the Center staff attached a note of its own explaining that participation in the study would in no way affect the refugee's standing with respect to employment, aid, or relocation.[14]

By using these procedures to select and contact members of the final sample, we hoped to obtain at least a 50 per cent turnout. We reasoned that the familiarity and respectability of the Refugee Center would at least partially counteract the very human tendency of the exiles to stay home when asked by strangers to venture out at night for an interview. Because we had neither the money nor the inclination to offer an attractive cash incentive to those who responded, we counted on our two letters, the

---

* We wanted the final sample to include only male heads of households because we were interested in factors affecting the decision to leave Cuba, and we wanted data from those presumed to be most involved in the decision.

prestige of the Center, and the "spirit" of the refugee community to secure the desired turnout. However, because the entire project had been set up by mail and telephone from a distance of 3,000 miles, and because we had had no previous personal contact with the Miami exile community, we were somewhat apprehensive as we set out for Florida.[15]

Our anxieties were soon dispelled. On the first of the four successive nights on which the selected Cubans had been invited to come to the Center, approximately 80 exiles came, and by the end of the final evening 211—or 53 per cent of the original 401 members of the sample—had reported to the Center and had received questionnaires.* The same administrative procedures were used each evening. Upon arriving at the Center, each exile was asked to relinquish his letter of invitation. Once seated in the large room where the questionnaires were administered, the exiles were greeted and given instructions in Spanish. We emphasized the nonofficial nature of the study and told them that we were interested in their opinions and experiences, that there were no "right" answers, that they were not to write their names on the questionnaires, and that strict anonymity would be maintained. Most respondents required from half an hour to an hour-and-a-half to complete the questionnaire, and it was the consensus of those present that the overwhelming majority of the respondents undertook the task with great seriousness and thoroughness.[16]

In addition to administering questionnaires to one group of refugees, we gathered data on several other groups. First, we obtained demographic information on a sample of relocated refugees—Cubans who had moved out of the Miami area and thus could not be represented in our final sample. Second, we

---

* Two persons were unable to fill in their questionnaires in a satisfactory manner; thus our subsequent analyses of the questionnaires are based on an N of 209. A comparison of the demographic characteristics of the respondents and the non-respondents (the 190 who did not appear at the Center) is included in Appendix B. The demographic data on non-respondents were taken from the master files of the Center.

obtained demographic information on the 190 members of the final sample who did not appear for any of the evening sessions. Third, we attempted to gather demographic information on all adults who had registered with the Center since its inception.*

We sought in addition to administer questionnaires to a number of "political activists" selected because they belonged to anti-Castro exile organizations. We did this because we had hypotheses about the behavior and attitudes of politically active exiles, and we were afraid that our systematic sample of heads of households would contain too few activists for comparative analysis. Contact was made with two anti-Castro organizations, one of which was a group of former pilots and the other a group called the *Movimiento Unidad Revolucionaria*. Questionnaires were given to both groups—although under less-than-optimal conditions. The pilots met at the home of one of the members and were given the questionnaire under our supervision. The members of the *MUR*, however, would not consent to such a gathering, and insisted on completing the forms on their own time; as a result, we had no control over the testing situation. A total of only 18 completed questionnaires was received. Subsequently, we found that our systematic sample included a sufficient number of political activists, and therefore responses from these 18 specially solicited questionnaires were not incorporated into our analysis.

In the chapters that follow, we present data on the refugees in cumulative fashion: each chapter incorporates data presented in the preceding chapters, in an attempt to construct a multivariable account of the manner in which certain Cubans were

* Eventually we were able to get all the data we needed on these groups, although when we left Miami only the data on the relocated refugees were actually complete. In Appendix B are tables that compare the distributions of four refugee groups on the variables age, occupation, education, and date of entry into the United States. The four groups are (1) a sample of all employable exile adults registered with the Center, (2) a sample of relocated adults, (3) those members of the final sample who completed the questionnaire, and (4) those members of the final sample who did not come to the Center and thus did not fill out the questionnaire.

brought to the irrevocable decision to leave their homeland. We begin in Chapter II with a demographic mapping of the community, indicating how the social characteristics of the exiles differ from those of Cubans in the home population. In Chapter III we examine refugee attitudes, with special attention being given to feelings about the revolution and the Castro government when it first came to power. Participation, both in the struggle against Batista and in anti-Castro activity, is the subject of Chapter IV. Chapter V presents data on the flow of refugees out of Cuba—on changes in the demography, attitudes, and political behavior of the refugees during the four-year period of emigration under study. The decision to leave is the subject of Chapter VI. There we discuss the types of experiences that first gave rise to dissatisfaction with the Castro regime and the types of subsequent experiences that precipitated the refugees into exile. In the final chapter we relate the process of citizen disillusionment and disaffection to the conduct and functioning of the Cuban Revolution.

II

Demography

Both critics and defenders of the Cuban revolution agree that those who have left the island do not represent a cross section of the total population. Of course, if one searches diligently enough, one can find representatives of all prerevolutionary social groups in the refugee community. There are illiterate campesinos and urban Negroes as well as former business executives and millionaires. But it is obvious to almost all concerned that a disproportionate number of refugees come from the middle and upper strata of prerevolutionary society.

Acknowledging this, however, does not commit us to any simplistic sociopolitical interpretation of the demography of the refugee community. For instance, it is quite incorrect to claim, as some have done, that those in exile come exclusively from the privileged sectors of the old Batistiano order and that they have fled the island with their ill-gotten gains. The "running dogs" of the old regime are in evidence in Miami, but only under the sponsorship of the Central Intelligence Agency at the time of the Bay of Pigs invasion did the most conservative groups achieve political dominance, and not since the earliest days of the exodus have they been in the majority. More sophisticated Cubans, both among those who have left and among those who have remained on the island, reject categorically such "theories" of exile, realizing that refugees from a revolution as complex, profound, and changeable as the Cuban have come from many social sectors and represent a variety of points of view.[1] At the very least, as will be noted in detail in Chapter III, events in Cuba precipitated many into exile who in 1959 had been fervent supporters of Castro. Thus, we can reject at the outset the notion that the refugee community represents either a cross section of the Cuban population or a simple exodus of members of the pre-Castro "establishment." The refugee flow is a consequence of the revolution, and because the revolution has meant different things at different times, the demographic composition of the refugee community has also been changing.

In this chapter we shall present an overview of the demographic characteristics of the refugee community considered as a whole at the end of 1962 and compare these characteristics with those of the home population. The primary source of data for these initial comparisons was a roster prepared by the Refugee Center in Miami, listing all previously employed or employable Cubans who had registered with the Center by March 1963. This roster contained data on 84,578 individuals classified according to occupation and month of entry into the United States. For purposes of our study, data on students, housewives, retired persons not classified by occupation, and all persons who entered the United States prior to the Castro take-over were removed from the roster. Our analysis is based on the remaining subpopulation of 59,682 individuals. Before proceeding, however, we must specify in more detail the relationship of this subpopulation to the total influx of Cubans.

It has been estimated that approximately 215,000 Cubans emigrated to the United States between the latter part of 1958 and the early part of 1963.[2] Approximately 165,000, or almost 77 per cent, registered with the Refugee Center in Miami. What do we know about the 23 per cent of the refugees who did not register with the Center and for whom we have no data? Do they differ in some systematic manner from those who did register? We must assume they do, but unfortunately we cannot specify the differences in great detail. However, two statements can be made with some certitude. First, those who did not register tend to be the more affluent and well-connected Cubans; the Center was established precisely to aid those who came with neither accumulated wealth nor immediate occupational plans. Second, those who did not register tend to come from among the refugees who arrived during the early months of the Castro regime; this is because the very affluent tended to leave first, and because the Refugee Center was not established until early in 1961. Furthermore, Cuban regulations governing the removal of money and possessions from the island did not become stringent until the middle of 1961.

Thus, the population we are analyzing underrepresents the early arrivals and the more wealthy refugees.[3] Where particular problems of analysis and inference suggest that this underrepresentation is especially important, we shall call attention to it. In general, however, we assume that an awareness on the part both of authors and of readers of this systematic bias is sufficient to caution all concerned against making any linear projections of our findings onto the entire refugee community.

What kinds of Cubans have fled to the United States? How do these exiles differ from those who have remained behind? The most powerful demographic variable for investigating these questions is occupation. When we compare the occupational distribution of Cubans, as indicated in the most recent pre-revolutionary Cuban census, with the occupational distribution of refugees, striking differences appear.[4] As can be seen in Table 2.1, professional and semiprofessional persons are overrepresented in the refugee community by a factor of more than five,[5] whereas persons engaged in agriculture and fishing are underrepresented by a factor of about 16. The other occupational types are distributed between these two extremes.[6]

TABLE 2.1

Occupational Comparison of Cuban Work Force and Cuban Refugees

Occupation	1953 Cuban Census	Percentage of Census	Cuban Refugees	Percentage of Refugees	Ratio: Percentage of Refugees to Percentage of Census
Lawyers and judges ..	7,858	.5%	1,695	3%	7.8
Professional and semi-professional	78,051	4	12,124	22	5.5
Managerial and executive	93,662	5	6,771	12	2.5
Clerical and sales	264,569	14	17,123	31	2.3
Domestic service, military, and police	160,406	8	4,801	9	1.1
Skilled, semiskilled, and unskilled	526,168	27	11,301	20	.75
Agricultural and fishing	807,514	41.5	1,539	3	.06
Total	1,938,228		55,354		

The occupational nonrepresentativeness of the refugees is reflected in the educational composition of the exile community. With 68 per cent of the employable refugees having white collar occupations, it is not surprising that more than one-third have at least completed high school. Table 2.2 compares the distribution of education in the total Cuban adult population (1953 census) with the distribution of education among the refugees.[7]

TABLE 2.2

Educational Comparison of Cuban Adults and Refugees

Education	Percentage of 1953 Cuban Census (N = 2,633,000)	Percentage of Refugees (N = 1,085)[a]
Less than fourth grade	52%	4%
Fourth grade to eleventh grade	44	60
Twelfth grade to three years of college	3	23.5
Four years of college or more	1	12.5

[a] The refugee data are taken from a systematic sample (by occupation) of the 59,682 individuals on the roster. The 1,096 refugees selected will hereafter be referred to as *the roster sample* in order to differentiate data derived from this sample from data derived from the entire roster. The sample size here is only 1,085 because educational data were not available for 11 persons.

Materials are available for one other comparison. Using the data in Table 2.3, we can estimate the average age of all adult Cubans in 1953 to be about 40.7 years and the average age of the employable refugees to be about 40.9.[8] Thus, there is almost no difference in average age between all adult Cubans and the refugees. However, the shapes of the two distributions are different. The descending order of the census distribution reflects a typical mortality curve, whereas the refugee distribution ascends to a peak in the 36–40 age bracket and then descends. Moreover, if a 1953 distribution of age of all employed Cubans were available, we would expect the average age of the employable refugees to be higher than the Cuban average. This is because refugees in those occupations that are overrepresented in Miami tend to be older than refugees in occupations that are underrepresented.

In order to extend our analysis to other variables, we must change the data base. The roster prepared by the Refugee Center includes data only on age, education, and prerevolutionary occupation. Using our survey of heads of households, we can compare the refugees and the home population with regard to income and place of residence. From what has been said about

TABLE 2.3

Age Distributions of Adult Cubans in 1953 and Employable Refugees

Age Group	1953 Census	Employable Refugees
21–25	17%	11%
26–30	14	12
31–35	13	13
36–40	12	16
41–45	11	15
46–50	9	11
51–55	7	8
56–60	4	7
61–65	5	3
66–70	3	2
71 and over	5	2

the occupations and the educational level of the employable adult refugees, one might expect our heads of households to have had considerable earning power in prerevolutionary Cuba. Such, in fact, was the case. When our respondents were asked how much money they had earned during 1958, the distribution shown in Table 2.4 was found. Grouping the data in this table, we see that approximately 23 per cent of our respondents earned less than $2,000, 56 per cent earned between $2,000 and $8,000, and 21 per cent earned more than $8,000. The average of the incomes reported was approximately $5,960, a figure that reflects the several very large incomes grouped in the table under the category "$15,000 or more."

It will be evident to anyone even vaguely familiar with prerevolutionary Cuba that neither this average income nor the income distribution reported in Table 2.4 was typical of that of the home population. The magnitude of the differences is suggested by the following: It is estimated that the gross national product per capita in Cuba was $431 in 1957.[9] With approximately one of every three Cubans employed, we can estimate the gross national product per working Cuban to have been about $1,293. If the refugees in our survey were representative of all working Cubans, they could be expected to have had an average annual income well *below* $1,293, because earned in-

TABLE 2.4

Income Earned in 1958 as Reported by Refugee Heads of Households

Income[a]	Percentage of Refugees Reporting (N = 199)
Less than $1,000	7%
$1,000 to 1,999	16
$2,000 to 3,999	27
$4,000 to 5,999	18
$6,000 to 7,999	11
$8,000 to 9,999	8
$10,000 to 14,000	7
$15,000 or more	6

[a] Income was reported in Cuban pesos. In 1958, one peso equaled one dollar.

come is only one of several components of gross national product. Instead, their average annual income exceeded this figure by a factor of more than four.

Another way of comparing the income distribution of the refugees to that of the home population is to look at the bottom end of the scale. A study done in Cuba in 1958 reported that 60.5 per cent of all employed males earned less than $900 a year.[10] On the other hand, only 7 per cent of the heads of households in our survey earned less than $1,000 in 1958. Clearly, the poorer sectors of Cuban society, which constitute a majority of the island's population, have contributed only marginally to the exodus.

To complete our demographic portrait of the refugees, we can make some comparisons with respect to place of residence in Cuba. The refugees in our sample were asked whether their homes had been in Havana, in some other large city, in a small city or town, or in the countryside. We did not define the terms "large city," "small city," or "the countryside," but rather let the respondent decide into which category his place of residence fell. The vagueness of these response categories makes comparisons with census categories difficult, but for purposes of Table 2.5, we have made the following assumptions: the response category "in Havana" is equivalent to the census category "greater Havana," the response category "some other large city" is equivalent to the census category "municipality of more that 50,000 inhabitants," "small city or town" is equivalent to the census category "municipality of more than 250 inhabitants but less than 50,000," and "the countryside" is equivalent to what the census denotes as "rural areas," that is, places of residence with fewer than 250 inhabitants and lacking basic urban services. When we compare the prerevolutionary urban-rural distribution of refugees with that of the home population, the differences are striking.[11] As can be seen, a disproportionate number of refugees come from Havana and other large cities. The inhabitants of rural areas, who comprise 43 per cent of the island's population, are almost unrepresented.

TABLE 2.5

Prerevolutionary Place of Residence of Refugees and of
Home Population

Place of Residence	Percentage of Refugees (N = 209)	Percentage of Home Population (N = 5,829,000)
In Havana	62%	21%
In some other large city	25	10
In a small city or town	11	26
In the countryside	2	43

The demographic data presented to this point indicate that the great preponderance of the refugees are drawn from the wealthier, the better educated, the more urban, and the higher occupational sectors. Once again, however, we must caution the reader that the sociological nonrepresentativeness of the refugee community does not indicate homogeneity of refugee origins or interests. There are enough bus drivers, mechanics, and shoe salesmen among the exiles to render simplistic class explanations of the exodus inaccurate. One of the most significant aspects of the Cuban revolution is that Cubans from so many walks of life were affected in ways that led to self-imposed exile. Although the refugee community contains the majority of living members of the Batistiano establishment, corrupt politicians, profiteers, landowners, and gangsters, most of the exiles come from the more inclusive social sectors that were squeezed, pressured, or deprived by the revolution not because their members wholeheartedly supported the old order, but because they stood in the way of the new. The Castro government became so radical and reorganized society so thoroughly that almost all social sectors from blue-collar workers through professionals experienced the impact of some revolutionary programs in a negative way. Of course, not all negative experiences with revolutionary programs resulted in self-imposed exile, both because of the counterbalancing effect of positive experiences and because of the psychological, physical, and political barriers to leaving the island. In terms of social structure, however, the range of "potential exiles" was very broad, eventually including all sectors of Cuban society except the rural masses. Above all, the flight of Cubans after 1959 cannot be interpreted as a departure of the privileged unless one is willing to define "the privileged" as all those who held steady jobs, ate decently, and wore shoes while Batista was in power.

Analysis of the demographic composition of the refugee community gives us some sense of the relative probability of self-imposed exile among various social sectors of pre-Castro Cuba, but it tells us little about the kinds of experiences that actually led to departure. As can be seen from the data in Table 2.1, for every lawyer and judge in exile in 1963, there were approximately five still in Cuba; and as one moves down the status hierarchy, increasingly larger percentages of each occupational group are seen to have remained behind. Demography helps to explain the propensity to leave, but the critical or precipitating factors are not demographic. What, then, are the other refugee characteristics and experiences that help to explain their exile? In the two chapters that follow we shall investigate attitudinal factors and patterns of political participation. As with demographic data, however, attitudinal and participation data contribute to our understanding of self-imposed exile without providing a full explanation. Only when we deal with the decision to leave Cuba, in Chapters V and VI, will a fuller explanation begin to emerge.

METHODOLOGICAL NOTE

In Chapter I, we argued that a sample of exile heads of households would provide sufficient data for a preliminary understanding of the processes that led individual Cubans to the decision to leave their homeland. For making generalizations about the Cuban refugee community in the aggregate, however, the sample of heads of households is clearly less satisfactory, both because of its small size and because of its special characteristics. Therefore, in constructing a composite demographic portrait of the refugees in Chapter II, wherever possible we have used data from the roster of employable exiles prepared by the Refugee Center. This data is augmented by materials taken from our survey. We follow this practice also in Chapter V, where we attempt to detail demographic and attitudinal changes among the exiles as these relate to date of departure from Cuba.

Because we combine data sources in these two chapters, we have the responsibility of specifying, wherever possible, the relationship between roster data and survey data. For instance, when we use survey data to estimate the prerevolutionary income distribution of exiles, we should attempt to answer such questions as "Do we get a profile that differs greatly from what we might have found had the roster itself contained data on income?" Although we cannot directly compare the survey sample and the roster employables with respect to income, we can suggest the magnitude and direction of possible errors by comparing them on the three demographic variables for which we have common data: age, education, and occupation. In so doing, we can gain some perspective on the extent to which our heads of households represent a skewed selection from among all adult employable refugees.*

First, consider the comparative distributions by age, given in Table 2.6. The data indicate that the heads of households in our survey tend to be older than the employable refugees.[12] The difference is most dramatic among those 25 or younger. As might be expected, there are very few heads of households in this age bracket. Although the differences reported in Table 2.6 are not

* In Appendix B we present analogous data, from which one may get some idea of the extent to which the heads of households in our survey represent (or fail to represent) an ideal sample of refugee heads of households. We include demographic data on two other groups: 179 heads of households who had been selected as part of our original sample but did not appear at the Refugee Center to fill out questionnaires, and a sample of 327 employable adults who had left the Miami area before our original sample was selected (March 1963).

TABLE 2.6

Comparative Age Distributions of Refugees on Roster Sample and
Heads of Households in Survey

Age	Roster Sample (N = 1,096)	Survey Sample (N = 209)
25 or younger	13%	4%
26 to 35	25	23
36 to 45	31	27.5
46 to 55	18	29
56 or older	13	16
No data	—	.5

large enough to suggest a reinterpretation of the income and place of residence analyses presented in this chapter, they should be kept in mind for future reference. Particularly in Chapters III and IV, where we discuss patterns of attitudes and of participation as a function of age, we consistently and of necessity underestimate the strength of relationships in the larger adult exile community by depending on data from heads of households, a sample that overrepresents the older age groups and underrepresents the young.

Next, consider the comparative educational distributions of the two groups, given in Table 2.7. At the university and professional levels there are almost no differences between the two groups; however, the heads of households sample contains a smaller percentage of individuals in the grammar school category and a larger percentage in the secondary school category than does the roster sample. In part, this reflects a non-response bias, because the heads of households in the original sample who did not submit to the questionnaire mirror the lower educational distribution of the roster more closely than those who responded (see Appendix B). In addition, a second factor is probably operative: In families with two or more employables, it is very likely that the head of household is the one with the highest level of education; thus a sample of heads of households would normally contain relatively fewer persons at the bottom of

TABLE 2.7

*Comparative Educational Distributions of Refugees on
Roster Sample and Heads of Households in Survey*

Education	Roster Sample (N = 1,096)	Survey Sample (N = 209)
Some grammar school[a]	45%	33%
Some secondary school[a]	31	42
Some university	12.5	12
Professional degree	10.5	10
No data	1	3

[a] The difference between the roster sample and the heads of households sample with respect to this category is significant at least at the .05 level using chi-square. The tests are based on two-by-two tables in which the upper two cells give the frequency of the indicated educational type in each of the two samples, and the lower two cells give the aggregate frequency of all the other educational types in the corresponding sample. Because the roster sample is so large, chi-square values tend to be rather high. That is, statistical significance is quite easy to achieve and too much importance should not be attached to these tests.

the educational scale than would a sample of all employable refugees. Once again, however, the differences between the two groups are not great. To the extent that income varies directly with education, using heads of households data to estimate income in the larger community results in a slightly inflated income figure, because of the overrepresentation of secondary school as compared to grammar school educations. But the inflationary tendency is certainly not very strong.

Finally, consider the comparative occupational distributions of the two groups, given in Table 2.8. The differences that appear in this table are not great and may well be a result of differences in coding. For instance, if we group the professionals, semiprofessionals, managers, and executives together, the percentage differences between the roster sample and the survey sample disappear. The same thing tends to happen if we group skilled labor with semiskilled and unskilled labor. It would seem that certain occupations that were classified as professional or skilled labor at the Refugee Center were classified by us as managerial and semiskilled, respectively. In any event, the two occupational distributions do not differ sufficiently to warrant

TABLE 2.8

*Comparative Occupational Distributions of Refugees on
Roster Sample and Heads of Households in Survey*

Occupation	Roster Sample (N = 1,096)	Survey Sample (N = 209)
Professional and semiprofessional[a]	23%[b]	16%
Managerial and executive[a]	13	22
Clerical and sales	31	25
Service	9	9
Skilled labor[a]	14	8
Semiskilled and unskilled labor[a]	7	11
Agricultural and fishing[a]	3	8
No data	1	1

[a] See note to Table 2.7, substituting "occupational" for "educational."
[b] These figures total more than 100 per cent because of rounding.

serious concern with the inaccuracies we may have introduced when estimating community characteristics (such as income and place of residence) from our sample of heads of households.

In summary, our comparison of the roster sample with the survey sample with respect to age, education, and occupation suggests that although differences exist, they are not of great magnitude or importance. When making inferences from the results of our survey to the larger community, we of course must exercise caution, particularly when using attitudinal and behavioral data; but the types of demographic bias that exist do not seem to be of either the scope or the magnitude that would invalidate or seriously weaken the inferences made in this and subsequent chapters.

III

Attitudes

As we have argued in the preceding chapter, the refugees, although by no means representative of the Cuban population, are nevertheless socially and demographically varied. Among those in our survey sample are lawyers and factory workers, large property owners and fishermen, young people in their twenties and old people in their seventies. There are some with little or no education who were barely able to scratch out answers to our questions, and others with professional degrees who wrote with force and polish. The diversity of the refugee community does not mirror the diversity of the home population, but it is sufficient to lead us to expect to find the attitudinal heterogeneity always found in groups that contain different social and educational strata.

This heterogeneity of attitudes is lessened somewhat by the fact that all are exiles. Because all have chosen to leave Cuba, almost all share in some degree certain resentments, longings, and disappointments. Except for the very few Cubans who went from a "good deal" under the Batista regime to an even "better deal" in the United States, the refugees abandoned their homeland with mixed feelings and, frequently, with heavy hearts.

Ninety-four per cent of those in our study reported that they had relatives in Cuba, and of these, 90 per cent said that the relatives were members of their immediate families. Almost all had left friends, jobs, and possessions behind, and remained attached both to particular people and places in Cuba and to their homeland in general. When we asked the members of our sample what aspects of their lives in Cuba they missed most, they responded largely in terms of family, jobs, and "the fatherland" (see Table 3.1).

As might be expected, despite ties to the island, refugee estrangement from the Castro regime is almost total. With the exception of two who did not respond to the question, all the exiles in our sample said that only the downfall of the existing government would lead them to return to Cuba.[1] When we asked the refugees about their present feelings toward Castro, 202 of the 204 responding described him as "one of the worst tyrants in the history of Cuba."[2] To a question concerning Castro's government, 91 per cent of those who responded said that it contained no honest and dedicated men.[3]

A further indication of exile rejection of the revolution and its leaders is presented in Table 3.2. We asked the refugees which Cubans had benefited most from the revolution. By put-

TABLE 3.1

Aspect of Past Life in Cuba Missed Most

Aspect of Life	Percentage of Refugees Responding (N = 209)
Family and homelife	38%[a]
"The fatherland"	25
Work or job	23
Security, amenities, and freedoms before the revolution	22
Customs, language, climate, friends, "the Cuban way of life"	18
Miscellaneous and "everything"	17
Nothing (or not responding)	4

[a] These figures total more than 100 per cent because of multiple responses.

TABLE 3.2

Cubans Who Have Benefited Most from the Revolution

Group or Sector	Percentage of Refugees Responding (N = 197)
No one	30%[a]
The Communists	32
The frustrated, the envious, opportunists, those of low moral character	32
Revolutionary leaders (excluding Castro)	8
Foreign Communists	7
Fidel Castro	7
Miscellaneous (pejorative)	2
The lower class	2

[a] These figures total more than 100 per cent because of multiple responses.

ting the question in positive terms, we hoped to increase the probability of receiving answers that connote at least partial admission of an improvement in life-style for some sectors of the population. However, as can be seen from the table, many exiles said that *no one* had benefited, and almost all the others responded by using terms that are clearly pejorative, such as "the Communists" or "the frustrated." Only three exiles mentioned the lower class, and none other than these three mentioned any group that might be considered worthy, attractive, or even neutral from the point of view of the refugees.

The fact that the refugees failed to respond in neutral or positive categories to our question about revolutionary benefits does not, however, indicate that they were unable to analyze the revolution in standard class and status terms. On the contrary, when asked which Cubans have been *hurt* most by the revolution, the exiles answered in more or less conventional fashion (see Table 3.3). The refugees reject the notion that "true" Cubans have benefited from the revolution: they feel that most of their countrymen have been hurt. In fact, the data in Table 3.3 underrepresent refugee feelings about the extent of social and political damage that has resulted from the revolu-

TABLE 3.3

Cubans Who Have Been Hurt Most by the Revolution

Group or Sector	Percentage of Refugees Responding (N = 202)
All Cubans	56%
All decent, honest, and/or hardworking persons	10
The workers	8
The middle class and/or property owners	6
All those desiring liberty, justice, and/or democracy	5
The lower classes	3
Children	2
Miscellaneous	10

tion. While selecting one group or sector as *most* hurt by the regime, respondents frequently emphasized that all other important sectors of the population had also been damaged. They saw themselves as pointing out only the worst casualties of Castro's rule.

Not only do the refugees reject the Castro regime, despise its leaders, and deny its accomplishments, they project their feelings onto the home population. When asked what percentage of Cubans would support a movement to overthrow the Castro government, three-fourths of the refugees replied that more than 70 per cent of the home population would be so inclined (see Table 3.4).

Similarly, the exiles project their almost unanimous hatred of Castro himself onto the home population. When asked who is the most hated man in Cuba, 92 per cent of the refugees responding named Castro.[4] Just as he has always been a symbol of the revolution to those who support it, Castro is its symbol—the devil incarnate—to those who oppose it.

In this atmosphere of total rejection of Castro and Castroism, what expectations prevail with regard to the future of Cuba? The exiles believe that a large majority of the home population would support a movement to overthrow the government, but

TABLE 3.4

Opposition to the Castro Regime Within the Cuban
Population as Estimated by Refugees

Estimated Percentage in Opposition	Percentage of Refugees Estimating (N = 203)
Less than 10%	.5%[a]
From 10 to 30%	2
From 30 to 50%	2.5
From 50 to 70%	20
From 70 to 90%	55
More than 90%	21

[a] These figures total more than 100 per cent because of rounding.

do they think that such an overthrow is probable? Apparently
not (or at least not in the short run). When we asked what the
immediate future holds in store for Cuba, a large majority saw a
continuation or worsening of present conditions, and only a few
predicted the end of the Castro government (see Table 3.5).[5]

Our study was done only a few months after the missile crisis
of October 1962, and less than two years after the failure of the
Bay of Pigs invasion. The general pessimism of the refugees
reflects in part the impact of these events, which demonstrated
both the high level of internal control maintained by the Castro
government and the unwillingness of the United States to inter-

TABLE 3.5

Predicted Changes in Cuba During the Next Two or Three Years

Predicted Changes	Percentage of Refugees Predicting (N = 198)
Increasing deterioration of the situation: more death, destruction, hunger, moral decadence, etc.	54%
Situation will worsen (no details mentioned)	18
End of Castro regime	13
Situation will remain unchanged	3
Impossible to say, and miscellaneous	12

vene with force sufficient to destroy the regime. Also reflected is the refugees' conviction that the regime is so evil that conditions can only get worse, as indicated in Table 3.5 by the large number of respondents who predicted increasing deterioration of conditions on the island over the next two or three years.

Up to this point, we have emphasized the homogeneity of refugee attitudes stemming from the common fact of exile. The picture that has been drawn is one of refugees still closely tied to certain social and symbolic aspects of their homeland, united in their hatred of Castro and his government, unwilling to admit that any "true" Cuban has benefited from the revolution, convinced that most of their countrymen despise Castro and are ready to support a movement to overthrow him, and quite pessimistic with respect to the possibility of a change of regime in the near future. Such is the cluster of attitudes that characterized our sample in the spring of 1963.

It is well known, however, that when Castro first came to power, he enjoyed the support and approval of great numbers of Cubans who subsequently left the island. A consequence of this shift from approval to disaffection is the frequently heard "betrayal" interpretation of the revolution. In its simplest form, this interpretation is that the democratic promises of Castro, combined with the tyranny of Batista, led most Cubans to support Castro prior to his assumption of power and even into the early years of his rule. Increasingly, however, the radicalization and eventual communization of the Cuban government alienated large sectors of the population. To the extent that members of these sectors expected one type of government and got quite another, they were betrayed by Castro and his lieutenants.[6]

Whether or not the supporters of Castro, now in exile, were *in some absolute sense* betrayed by the regime is of little or no importance to our analysis. In fact they expected one type of government, and in fact they got quite another. For those who believed fervently in Castro when he was in the Sierra fighting against Batista, but later came to reject his regime in its entirety, the psychological stresses must have been very great indeed. The expectations they held before Castro assumed power were shattered in 1959 and the early 1960's, and that they should *perceive* themselves as having been betrayed is, for our purposes, the salient psychological fact. We assume that those exiles who at one time supported Castro and later came to despise him differ in important ways from those who had less positive feelings about him from the outset; we leave to others the problem of whether or not they were in any real sense betrayed. It is sufficient for our purposes to note that they probably went through an agonizing process of disillusionment.

When we attempt to identify the members of our sample who at one time supported Castro, we encounter a serious methodological problem. As we have already shown, the refugees unanimously reject the Castro regime. Because of the strength of their feelings and the general hostility of the community toward all things associated with Castro, we knew that our respondents would find it difficult to admit that they had ever entertained positive feelings toward him or his government. To do so would run counter to important norms of the exile community, and for many refugees would amount to a confession of having been "tricked" or "duped" in the early years. Furthermore, four years had passed since Castro's assumption of power, and the strength of early enthusiasms had undoubtedly been partially forgotten or repressed under the pressure of intervening events. To ask someone how he felt four years ago is never a very satisfactory research technique, and in the case of the refugees it was perhaps less satisfactory than usual.

Nevertheless, we saw no alternative to asking retrospective questions. To make the data manageable and to minimize error we combined responses to these questions on a single scale indicating the refugees' initial attitude toward the revolution.[7] The scale was constructed from the following questions and responses:

11. Think back to 1958 when Batista was still in power. How did you feel toward the Batista government at that time?[8]
    I agreed with many of the Batista government's policies.
    I agreed with some of the Batista government's policies.
    I agreed with a few of its policies.
    I agreed with none of its policies.
    I hated the Batista tyranny.

13. When Castro first took over in 1959, which of the following best describes your feelings toward him at that time?
    I thought he was the savior of Cuba.
    I admired him a great deal.
    I admired him some.
    I admired him very little.
    I did not admire him at all.

14. *During the first six months of 1959*, did Castro work toward accomplishing his announced aims and programs?
    Yes, he worked *very* hard.
    Yes, he made some effort.
    Yes, he made a little effort.
    No, he made no effort at all.

15. How did you feel about the *revolutionary government* in general when it first came to power in 1959?
    I felt very strongly that it was composed of honest and dedicated men.
    I felt that it contained many honest and dedicated men.
    I felt that it contained a few honest and dedicated men.
    I felt that it contained no honest and dedicated men.

Of our 209 respondents, approximately 11 per cent scored four points, the number indicating the most favorable attitude toward the revolution. The remainder of the sample was distributed approximately as follows: 23 per cent scored three, 27 per cent scored two, 23 per cent scored one, and 16 per cent scored zero. Because the numbering system of such scales is arbitrary, it should be emphasized that even a score of zero may indicate some slight approval of the revolution in 1959. In general, increasing scores should be understood to mean a progression from very minimal initial approval of the revolution to very strong support. The degree of support among the members of our sample is perhaps more precisely indicated by the fact that approximately 22 per cent of those responding said that in 1959 they had felt that Castro was the savior of Cuba, and approximately 16 per cent had felt very strongly at that time that the revolutionary government was composed of honest and dedicated men.[9]

In the analyses that follow, we will use this scale of initial attitude toward the revolution without constantly reminding the reader of its limitations. The fact that it probably underestimates the true level of initial approval of the revolution among the refugees is not very important for our purposes. We are interested in determining how those who were initially more favorable toward the revolution differ from those who were initially less favorable rather than in estimating the overall level of support that once existed among those now in exile.[10]

When we examine the refugees' initial attitudes toward the revolution in the light of the demographic variables introduced in Chapter II, a consistent but complex pattern emerges. As shown in Table 3.6, there is a direct relationship between youth and a more favorable initial view of the revolution. Refugees 35 years of age and younger were more favorably disposed toward the revolution than were those from 36 to 50. Similarly, those from 36 to 50 were more favorably disposed than those

TABLE 3.6

Initial Attitudes Toward the Revolution by Age

	Ages of Respondents		
Attitudes	35 and Younger (N = 55)	36–50 (N = 86)	51 and Older (N = 67)
Less favorable[a]	47%	62%	87%
More favorable	53	38	13
Chi-square = 21.9		$p < .001$	

[a] In this, as in all subsequent dichotomizations of the scale on initial attitude toward the revolution, scale types zero, one, and two have been grouped together as less favorable, and types three and four have been grouped together as more favorable.

51 and older. In this instance, it would seem, we find a reflection in the refugee population of the situation that prevailed in Cuba during the first year or two of the Castro government. Lloyd Free, in a study conducted in Cuba in 1960, found that younger people were disproportionately represented among those adult Cubans whom he classified as supporters of the regime.[11] Of course, the level of initial support for the revolution was undoubtedly lower among exiles in all age groups than it was in the general population. However, the pattern of support by generation is similar, underlining the special role that youth played in the "struggle against the tyranny" of the Batista regime. In both the refugee population and the home population we see the classic relationship between the young and anti–status quo movements.[12]

When we consider the relation of the educational level of Cubans to early support for the revolution, we find that the pattern characteristic of the Cuban home population is reversed among the exiles. Free found that 90 per cent of those Cubans with elementary educations or no schooling supported the regime, while the level of support dropped to 83 per cent among those with secondary educations. The lowest level of support, 77 per cent, was found among those who had attended universities.[13] On the other hand, in our refugee sample there is a direct, rather than inverse, relationship between higher levels of education and more favorable attitudes toward the revolution in 1959. The association is not strong, but it is consistent across all three educational groups (see Table 3.7).

Free's finding that the less educated Cubans in the home population tended to show higher levels of support for the revolution is fairly easy to explain. The reforms undertaken by Castro in 1959 and early 1960 had a class bias in that they benefited most directly those who were lower in the socioeconomic hierarchy. Government programs to promote the reduction of rents and utility rates, land reform, and the expropriation of certain properties were very favorably received by Cubans in

TABLE 3.7

Initial Attitudes Toward the Revolution by Educational Level

	Educational Levels of Respondents		
Attitudes	Some Primary School (N = 68)	Some Secondary School (N = 88)	Some University (N = 47)
Less favorable	74%	64%	55%
More favorable	26	36	45
Chi-square = 4.18		$p < .20$	

the lower and even the middle levels of society. Free found that support for the revolutionary government increased from 71 per cent in the upper and upper-middle socioeconomic groups to 87 per cent in the lower-middle group, and finally to 90 per cent in the lowest group.[14] Because educational level correlates very highly with socioeconomic standing in the home population, the pattern of support by educational groups mirrors the pattern of support by socioeconomic groups.

The situation in the refugee community, however, is different. Among the refugees, differences in prerevolutionary income between educational groups were not as great as they were in the home population. Refugees with higher education tended to have high incomes before the revolution, of course, but the income levels of the middle and lower educational groups were relatively high as well. For instance, 40 per cent of the refugees with some primary education had earned from $3,000 to $8,000 in 1958, and 9 per cent had earned more than $8,000. Among those with some secondary education, the comparable figures are respectively 42 per cent and 22 per cent. Among those with some university education, 40 per cent had earned from $3,000 to $8,000, and 40 per cent had earned more than $8,000. Clearly, the less educated refugees, although not as well-off financially as their well-educated counterparts, were unusually prosperous when compared with typical Cubans of lower education. Among the refugees are a disproportionate number of

Table 3.8
Initial Attitudes Toward the Revolution Among Educational Groups by Age

Attitudes	Some Primary School			Some Secondary School			Some University		
	35 or Younger (N = 10)	36-50 (N = 31)	51 or Older (N = 26)	35 or Younger (N = 27)	36-50 (N = 36)	51 or Older (N = 25)	35 or Younger (N = 16)	36-50 (N = 19)	51 or Older (N = 12)
Less favorable	60%	68%	85%	48%	64%	80%	31%	47%	100%
More favorable	40	32	15	52	36	20	69	53	0

Chi-square = 27.49 $p < .001$

self-made men, men of little formal training who were doing
very well as merchants, landlords, military men, and even skilled
laborers when Castro came to power. Their presence in the survey sample should caution us against attempting to infer the
socioeconomic status of the refugees directly from their educational level.[15]

We still have not, however, explained why there should be a
positive relationship in the refugee sample between education
and initial support for the revolution. Of several factors that
seem to be operative, one is the influence of age on education.
That is, we have shown that the younger refugees were more
favorably disposed toward the revolution than were the older
exiles. We also know that the younger refugees, in general, have
a higher level of education. For instance, 30 per cent of those in
the youngest group have had some university training. In the
middle group the figure drops to 22 per cent, and among those
51 or older, only 19 per cent have attended a university. Thus,
the young are overrepresented among the university-educated
refugees and underrepresented among those with only primary
schooling.

The educational differences between age groups are small,
however, and we would therefore expect educational level to
have an effect on attitudes toward the revolution in 1959 independent of age. In other words, not only would we expect to find
the younger refugees within each educational group more favorable in their initial attitudes toward the revolution than the
older refugees, we would also expect to find an increase in
favorable attitudes within each generation as we move up the
educational hierarchy. Table 3.8 clarifies the relationships between age, education, and initial attitude toward the revolution.
Within each educational group, the level of initial support for
the revolution can be seen to decrease as age increases. The
pattern is consistent, and most pronounced in the university
group, where among those 51 and older there are no refugees
with "more favorable" attitudes toward the revolution. It is im-

portant to note also that higher education has a positive influence on attitudes toward the revolution independent of age. That is, among refugees 35 or younger, those with university educations were more favorable than those with secondary educations, and those with secondary educations were more favorable than those with primary schooling. The same pattern is apparent within the group whose members range in age from 36 to 50. Among those 51 or older, however, the pattern is irregular, with the most educated having the least favorable initial attitudes.

This educational patterning within age groups suggests a complex demographic relationship among the exiles in terms of initial support for the revolution. Those who were both young and highly educated were by far the most favorable group in 1959. As university students or recent graduates during the struggle against Batista, they were the most politically aware of the younger generation, the most intimately tied to pro-Castro movements and the politics of reform. Subsequently, they traveled the longest and perhaps the most tortuous road in the process of disillusion and disaffection. On the other hand, the oldest and best-educated group of exiles was the least favorable toward the revolution from the outset. Having had university training, they—like their younger counterparts—paid a great deal of attention to the political life of Cuba in the fifties. However, the rise of Castro and the fall of Batista affected them in quite a different manner. While few of them were full-fledged Batistianos, they nevertheless belonged to those social sectors that were prospering under the old regime. Although their student sons and daughters may have been in full ideological rebellion against Batista, they themselves were closely tied to the status quo. They were relatively wealthy, educated, and well connected, and probably quite cynical with regard to corruption and tyranny in government. Castro appeared to them not as the savior of Cuba, but rather as a troublesome and radical young man whose followers destroyed property, interrupted urban services, and succeeded only in goading Batista into certain "excesses" that did not make particularly pleasant table conversation.

One point remains to be made. In Table 3.8 it was shown that in the middle and lower educational groups, both age and amount of schooling directly affected the level of initial support for the revolution. Although the differences were not great, in each age group those with less education were less likely to have indicated support. In our attempt to explain this pattern we have found occupational data helpful. In Table 3.9 exile occupational groups are listed in descending order, from those that were initially most favorable to those that were least favorable. The differences are not dramatic, but they are suggestive. The military and police group falls entirely into the "less favorable" category. Next among the least favorable groups are those in agriculture and fishing. Together these two groups contain almost 15 per cent of our sample, and in both the educational level is relatively low. Refugees who were members of the military and police services were opposed to the revolution because of occupational connections with the Batista government. Refugees from the agricultural sector were largely opposed to Castro from the beginning; they were primarily rural landowners who had anticipated the events that would follow a Castro takeover

TABLE 3.9

Attitudes Toward the Revolution in 1959 by Occupational Groups

Occupational Group	Percentage of Members More Favorable	Percentage of Members Less Favorable
Semiskilled and unskilled (N = 29)	45%	55%
Clerical and sales (N = 53)	40	60
Skilled labor (N = 16)	37	63
Professional and semiprofessional (N = 33)	33	67
Managerial and executive (N = 46)	33	67
Agricultural and fishing (N = 17)	24	76
Military and police (N = 13)	0	100

even when he was in the Sierra, or who had suffered under the agrarian reform of 1959. Although they are classified as "agricultural," they should not be thought of as peasants. Most of them come from the stratum of rural farmers and ranchers that was poorly educated but relatively successful in financial terms.

At the other extreme, the three occupational groups whose members most favored the revolution were the semiskilled and unskilled workers, those in clerical and sales work, and skilled workers. In general, members of these groups are from Havana or other large cities. Although not as well educated as the professionals and the executives, they tend to be better educated than members of the agricultural and military groups. In the higher levels of initial support manifested by those with some secondary education, one can see the influence of these three occupational groups, especially the 25 per cent of our sample who were in clerical and sales work when Castro came to power.

In the second half of this chapter we have tried to indicate what types of exiles were initially most favorable toward the revolution. Given the fact that the exiles were unanimous in rejecting the revolution in 1963, while their attitudes were quite diverse in 1959, it seems reasonable to assume that those who were initially most favorable experienced a very complex and trying process of disaffection and disillusion. Thus—to cite two extremes—a university student who believed in 1959 that Castro was the savior of Cuba undoubtedly came to exile by a different path than an elderly lawyer who distrusted Castro and his lieutenants from the outset. It should be clear from the foregoing discussion, however, that we are not attempting to infer the distribution of support for Castro among Cubans in 1959 from our refugee data. Although there are similarities in the patterns of refugee support and the patterns of home-population support that existed at the outset of the revolution, the differences are at least as important as the similarities.

METHODOLOGICAL NOTE

In dealing with similarities and differences in exile attitudes, we feared that a systematic bias might be introduced as a result of the special circumstances both of refugee residence in the United States and of the interview situation itself. That is, most Cuban exiles have come to the United States without visas (i.e., as parolees), all our respondents had accepted some form of aid from the Refugee Center, and many were receiving relief payments. Moreover, the fact that the refugees in our sample were asked to come to the Center to fill out their questionnaires gave the proceedings a semiofficial aura that our disclaimers could not entirely remove. We were running the risk, it seemed, of eliciting from our respondents answers reflecting their perceptions of what we might want them to say. In short, we were concerned about the problem of flattery discussed by Alex Inkeles and Raymond Bauer in *The Soviet Citizen* (Cambridge, Mass., 1959). We wanted some check on the possibility that the refugees, thinking of themselves as guests of the government and perceiving us as its representatives, might exaggerate their admiration of the United States in a way that would relate systematically to their other opinions.

To investigate the problem of systematic bias resulting from flattery, we constructed a Guttman scale from responses (strongly agree, agree, indifferent, disagree, strongly disagree) to the following five assertions (question 35):

> During the last 50 years, the United States has interfered too much in the *political* affairs of Cuba.
> During the last 50 years, the United States has interfered too much in the *economic* affairs of Cuba.
> During the Batista days, many United States *tourists* behaved badly when visiting Cuba.
> During the Batista days, many United States *businessmen* behaved badly when visiting Cuba.
> The government of the United States has always been in the right in its relations with Castro.

Of our 209 respondents, approximately 9 per cent scored five points on the scale, the number indicating the most critical attitude toward the United States. The remainder was distributed approximately as follows: 7 per cent scored four, 19 per cent scored three, 25 per cent scored two, 26 per cent scored one, and 14 per cent scored zero. (Details of scale construction are given in Appendix B.) As we noted with regard to the scale on attitude toward the revolution in 1959, this number system may be misleading. In this case, even those scoring one gave at least one response that is critical of the United States; only those scoring zero gave no critical responses. The absolute level of criticism is suggested by the fact that 34 per cent of those responding said they agreed or strongly agreed that the U.S. had interfered too much in the political affairs of Cuba, and 41 per cent of those responding disagreed or strongly disagreed with the assertion that the U.S. has always been in the right in its relations with Castro.

Taken by itself, this scale does not demonstrate the absence of flattery. It is highly probable that our sample contains a fair number of individuals who, despite their true feelings, hesitated to criticize the United States while being questioned by citizens of that country and enjoying the hospitality and facilities of the Refugee Center. However, we found that scores on the criticism scale are unrelated to *any* of the key variables with which this study deals. For instance, there is no significant relationship between criticism of the United States and attitude toward the revolution in 1959. (The criticism scale was dichotomized, in this and in all subsequent instances, by grouping zero, one, and two together as "less critical," and three, four, and five together as "more critical." The statistical test of association used in all analyses involving the criticism scale is chi-square. When we speak of finding "no significant relationship" we mean that $p > .10$). Similarly, there is no significant relationship between criticism of the United States and any of the following variables: participation in the struggle against Batista (introduced in

Chapter IV), the dates on which the refugees decided to depart from Cuba (1960 or earlier as opposed to 1961 or later—a variable used in Chapter V), age (45 or younger as opposed to 46 or older), education (those who were not high school graduates as opposed to those who were), and employment status ("currently employed" as opposed to "on relief or unemployed").

In all our tests involving the criticism scale, we found that it related to only one other variable. We asked the refugees (question 25) what had disappointed them most about the United States since their arrival. Seventy of the 196 responding to this question said that nothing had disappointed them; the others mentioned a wide variety of experiences and problems. The 70 who said that nothing had disappointed them were more likely ($p < .10$) than the others to come from the group scoring low on criticism of the United States. Because of obvious similarities in the disappointment and criticism dimensions, we consider this finding nothing more than a validation of the criticism scale itself.

Thus, although there may well be flatterers (defined as those who criticized the United States less than they would under most other circumstances) among our respondents, flattery as a variable does not relate to other important variables. This would suggest that no systematic bias is introduced by this aspect of the context of our research. The evidence indicates that any flatterers that might exist are distributed randomly through our sample.

IV

Political Participation

We know from the extensive literature on political behavior that although attitudes predispose individuals toward political action, attitudes in themselves do not determine behavior. For every civil rights worker in the United States there are hundreds who are sympathetic to the cause but do not lift a finger; for every contributor to a political campaign there are dozens who believe in the candidate but do not give a cent; and for every Republican and Democratic voter there is usually a third citizen who has favorable opinions about one or the other party but who never gets to the voting booth. Between the opinion and the act are a great many hurdles—some psychological, some sociological, and some political. So wide is the gulf between having opinions and taking action that during normal times the only overt form of political participation engaged in by the vast majority of citizens in the United States and other countries is voting.[1] In systems without elections, the majority, as a rule, cannot be said to participate in the political process at all.

Under certain conditions, however, particularly when a system is under great stress, the complex of psychological, sociological, and political factors that usually insulates the citizen from all forms of participation other than voting breaks down. Under such conditions, affect runs high, motivations are quickened, goals are restructured, new opportunities for action present themselves, and very frequently new leadership emerges. In times of great stress there is sometimes mass political participation that is quite different both in intensity and in content from the usual order of activity.

During the last years of Batista's rule, and particularly during 1958, such conditions came to prevail in Cuba. Although the island was never wracked by full-scale civil war, popular revulsion against the dictatorship was widespread, and many otherwise noninvolved Cubans began to help the rebel cause in one way or another. (Aiding the rebel cause did not necessarily mean aiding Castro, for there were other groups working against Batista.)[2] It is impossible to estimate the extent of anti-Batista activity, but most responsible observers agree that at least in the major cities large sectors of the adult population gave some form of aid and comfort to the revolutionaries.[3] In this chapter we shall examine the distribution of anti-Batista and subsequent anti-Castro activity among those Cubans who are now in exile. Our primary purpose in so doing is not to make inferences about the distribution of such activity in the home population, but to identify those Cubans who participated in the revolt against Batista and now find themselves in exile and in total opposition to his successor.*

In Chapter III we saw that according to our scale of "initial attitude toward the revolution" almost every member of the survey sample admitted having favored the revolution in 1959 to at least some degree. At the lower end of the scale, the degree

---

* It is important to note, however, that the exiles in our survey—coming as they do from the more urban, literate, and politically aware sectors of the population—may well display an aggregate profile of anti-Batista activity that reflects rather closely the situation in Cuba in 1957 and 1958. With the exception of some peasants active in the Sierra Maestra and later in the Escambray, the majority of the Cubans working against Batista were from the urban, literate, and politically aware sectors of the population.

of approval was very small, of course. Nevertheless, our data suggest that there once existed among Cubans now in exile a vast reservoir of anti-Batista and pro-revolutionary sentiment. We would expect some subpopulation of these refugees to have worked actively for the rebel cause, and we would expect to find that members of this subpopulation (henceforth called "participants") were recruited predominantly from among those refugees who had more favorable initial attitudes toward the revolution. However, we would also expect to find some participants among those who were initially less favorable. As in so many other political situations, the "lesser of two evils" rationale operated in some sectors of Cuban society in 1957 and 1958. Many Cubans who were only lukewarm toward Castro considered him potentially an improvement over Batista.[4] Normally, such lukewarm feelings would not have moved them to support revolutionary activity, but conditions in urban Cuba during this period were far from normal. Because the civic resistance against Batista was efficiently organized and because many of the requests it made of the citizens—such as those for donations of money to help the rebel cause—were fairly easy to comply with, many Cubans who were not emotionally caught up in the struggle against Batista nevertheless took action that qualified them as participants.

Before beginning our attitudinal and demographic analysis of participant refugees, we must indicate how we defined participation for purposes of this study. We asked our respondents (question 12) if, before Castro came to power, they had helped him or the revolutionary cause in any way. If they said they had, we asked them what specific action or actions they had taken.[5] The distribution of their responses is given in Table 4.1. As can be seen in the table, one of every three refugees said that he had aided the rebel cause in some way. From the data reported in this table, we constructed an index of participation. Fighting openly against the Batista regime was scored as three points, working in or with the underground was scored as two

TABLE 4.1

Refugee Participation in Anti-Batista Activity

Type of Activity	Percentage of Refugees (N = 209)
None	67%[a]
Contributed money	23
Worked in or with the underground	12
Contributed supplies or other services	7
Other help or contribution	5
Fought openly against the Batista regime	1

[a] These figures total more than 100 per cent because of multiple responses among those who participated.

points, and all other forms of participation were scored as one point each. A total score was then calculated for each participant by adding the points assigned him for each activity in which he had engaged. The highest possible score on this index was eight points (three for fighting, two for working in or with the underground, and one each for contributing money, supplies, and other forms of help). None of the participants scored eight points, however, nor were there any who scored seven (see Table 4.2). As is predictable from the data in Table 4.1, most participants scored only one point.

TABLE 4.2

Distribution of Participation Scores of Refugees Active in the Struggle Against Batista

Index of Participation	Number of Refugees
1	37
2	16
3	9
4	5
5	1
6	1
Total	69

To return to the relationship between initial attitudes toward
the revolution and participation in anti-Batista activity, we can
restate our hypothesis as follows: The more favorable a refugee's initial attitude toward the revolution, the higher the probability that he was a participant. As noted earlier, because almost all the refugees expressed at least slight approval of some
aspect of the revolution at its beginning, we would expect to
find some participants even among those who were least favorable. But certainly the majority of participants should be found
among the refugees whose attitudes were more favorable. In
Table 4.3 we present data relevant to this hypothesis. The scale
of initial attitudes toward the revolution, dichotomized in
Chapter III, is here trichotomized: those who scored zero are
grouped together as *least favorable,* those who scored one or
two are grouped together as *more favorable,* and those who
scored three or four are grouped together as *most favorable.*
As can be seen, the association between initial attitude toward
the revolution and participation in support of the rebels is extremely strong. Of particular interest is the finding that there
were *no* participants among those whose attitudes were classified as least favorable (those who scored zero on the initial attitude scale). Evidently, the very slight initial approval of the
revolutionary movement that is characteristic of this group was
not sufficient to lead to pro-rebel activity.

We can extend our analysis of the relationship between at-

TABLE 4.3

*Participation in Anti-Batista Activity by Initial
Attitude Toward the Revolution*

	Initial Attitudes Toward the Revolution		
Participation	Least Favorable (N = 34)	More Favorable (N = 104)	Most Favorable (N = 71)
Participated	0%	22%	65%
Did not participate	100	78	35
Chi-square = 54.8		p < .001	

TABLE 4.4

*Level of Participation in Anti-Batista Activity by Initial
Attitude Toward the Revolution (Participants Only)*

Level of Participation	Initial Attitudes Toward the Revolution	
	More Favorable (N = 23)	Most Favorable (N = 46)
High	30%	54%
Low	70	46
Chi-square = 3.53	p < .10	

titudes and participation by dividing the participants into two types—those who scored only one point on the index of participation and those who scored two or more. We find that the most active participants came primarily from the group initially most favorable toward the revolution (see Table 4.4).

Because the association between attitudes and participation reported in Table 4.3 is so strong, it is not surprising to find that there is also a strong relationship between age and participation. In Chapter III it was shown that the young refugees were much more likely than their older counterparts to have had favorable attitudes toward the revolution in 1959. Much the same relationship holds between age and participation.* In Table 4.5 we can see that as we move up through the generations there are increasingly smaller percentages of participants in each age group.

On the other hand, the relationship between education and participation does not follow so exactly the pattern between education and initial attitudes described in Chapter III. There we found a weak, positive relationship between education and initial attitudes. That is, the higher the level of education the more favorable the attitude toward the revolution. Similarly,

* In Chapter III we argued that the relationship between age and attitudes in the refugee population reflects a general pattern in the home population. It seems reasonable to assume that much the same argument would hold for the relationship between age and participation.

TABLE 4.5

Participation in Anti-Batista Activity by Age

	Ages of Respondents		
Participation	35 or Younger (N = 55)	36–50 (N = 86)	51 or Older (N = 67)
Participated	51%	35%	16%
Did not participate	49	65	84
Chi-square = 16.4		p < .001	

as we move up the educational hierarchy, we find a higher percentage of participants in each successive group. The differences in this case, however, are slight, and none reaches statistical significance. However, if we confine our analysis to those who participated, the relationship is stronger. This is shown in Table 4.6, where the 69 participants are again separated into those who were more active and those who were less active. We find that there is a positive relationship between high participation and a higher level of education. It would seem that among the refugees, participants were drawn from all educational levels, but those who participated most tended to be those with more education. This is consistent with what is known about anti-Batista activity in Cuba: The urban resistance drew active support from individuals in almost all social sectors, but those with higher levels of education had skills and resources that

TABLE 4.6

Level of Participation in Anti-Batista Activity
by Education (Participants Only)

	Education	
Level of Participation	Some Secondary (N = 34)	Finished Secondary (N = 35)
High	35%	57%
Low	65	43
Chi-square = 3.31	p < .10	

enabled them to make a contribution that was out of proportion to their numbers.

In the distribution of participation by occupation, we can
also see the diversified bases of support enjoyed by the rebels.
With the exception of the military and the police, all of whom
were directly in the service of Batista, none of the refugee occupational groups had more than 44 per cent or less than 30
per cent of its members engaged in pro-rebel activity (see
Table 4.7). With regard to participation in anti-Batista activity
by occupational groups, we hypothesize that the distribution we
have found among the refugees reflects in some rough fashion
the general behavior of the urban sectors in pre-Castro Cuba.

To this point we have concentrated on relating anti-Batista
participation to the demography of the refugees. We have seen
that the close association of more favorable initial attitudes
toward the revolution and participation in anti-Batista activities leads to a profile of the participant refugee that is quite
similar to the profile of the initially pro-Castro refugee.

With this background in mind, let us turn to the question of
longitudinal political activity among the refugees. By "longitudinal political activity" we mean the relationship between participation in anti-Batista activities in the late 1950's and participation in anti-Castro activities at some later date. At first

TABLE 4.7

Participation in Anti-Batista Activity by Occupational Groups

Occupational Group	Percentage of Members that Participated	Percentage of Members that Did Not Participate
Skilled labor (N = 16)	44%	56%
Semiskilled and unskilled (N = 29)	41	59
Managerial and executive (N = 46)	41	59
Clerical and sales (N = 53)	30	70
Professional and semiprofessional (N = 33)	30	70
Agricultural and fishing (N = 17)	30	70
Military and police (N = 13)	0	100

glance, it is tempting to advance what might be called the "continuing participant" hypothesis. Briefly, the argument would go as follows: The predominantly young and relatively well-educated refugees who participated in the struggle against Batista would be more likely than other refugees to engage in anti-Castro activity once in exile. There are two reasons for this. First, they are more likely to be "participant types" who cannot stand idly by in the face of perceived political wrongdoing. They are activists by upbringing and experience, politically conscious and involved. Just as they were recruited to fight against Batista, the probability is high that they can be recruited for the fight against Castro once they come to perceive him as an enemy of the fatherland. Second, it is precisely the participants in the fight against Batista who have undergone the most agonizing process of disillusionment and disaffection. Because they once believed in the revolutionary cause and invested their time and energy in aiding it, their frustration and anger in exile is greater than that of other refugees. Spurred on by a redemptive urge and anxious to get even with "Castro the betrayer," they would naturally be quick to engage in activities designed to weaken or overthrow the regime.

As reasonable as this argument seems, it is only weakly supported by our data. We asked each of our respondents (question 36) if he had been active in any Cuban refugee organization since coming to the United States. If he said yes, we asked him the name of the organization and the nature of his participation. Of the 209 members of the survey sample, 58 had been or were at the time of the survey active in some sort of exile organization. Although those who belonged to exile organizations tended to come in disproportionate numbers from among those who had participated in anti-Batista activity, the tendency was not statistically significant.

We were able to see in retrospect, however, that these data do not provide a very convincing test of the continuing participant hypothesis. By asking about membership in exile organizations rather than asking directly about participation in anti-Castro activity, we introduced extraneous factors. Some exiles belonged to professional or fraternal organizations concerned primarily with the maintenance of group identification rather than with the overthrow of Castro. Other refugees had joined the armed forces of the United States and reported this as organizational membership. Additionally, there were probably many respondents who were engaged in anti-Castro activities without being members of exile organizations. In sum, our question concerning membership in exile organizations provided an inaccurate measure of exile participation in anti-Castro activity.

We attempted a second test of the continuing participant hypothesis by separating out, from among all the refugees who reported membership in exile organizations, those who belonged to *political* organizations. Political organizations were defined as groups identified by knowledgeable informants as specifically dedicated to the overthrow of the Castro government. Respondents affiliated with such organizations will hereafter be termed "politically active" refugees, for we can safely consider them to have been engaged in overt anti-Castro behavior. Undoubtedly, many refugees without such membership were similarly engaged, but with our data we cannot identify them with any precision. As can be seen in Table 4.8, when the

TABLE 4.8

*Comparison of Politically Active and Other Refugees
with Respect to Anti-Batista Activity*

Participation in Anti-Batista Activity	Politically Active in Exile (N = 30)	Politically Inactive in Exile[a] (N = 179)
Participated	47%	31%
Did not participate	53	69
Chi-square = 2.95	$p < .10$	

[a] As noted in the text, this category includes many refugees who were politically active but whom we cannot identify as such.

politically active refugees are compared to the other refugees
in the survey sample with respect to prior participation in anti-
Batista activity, the continuing participant hypothesis is supported, albeit weakly.[6]

One further comparison is possible. Let us return for a moment to the group of 58 refugees who reported that they were
active in some sort of exile organization. If we compare the 30
politically active refugees with the remaining 28 refugees (those
who were active in nonpolitical organizations) with regard to
their initial attitudes toward the revolution, an interesting association is found. As shown in Table 4.9, the members of nonpolitical organizations were recruited overwhelmingly from
those with less favorable initial attitudes toward the revolution,
while nearly half the politically active exiles had more favorable
initial attitudes. To state the relationship in another fashion,
those refugees who were lukewarm toward the revolution from
the outset tended to join nonpolitical organizations in exile if
they entered any at all, while those who strongly favored the
revolution in 1959 tended to join political organizations. Thus,
both participation in the struggle against Batista and participation in anti-Castro activity while in exile tend to be related to
initial attitude toward the revolution.

We cannot discuss longitudinal participation any further on
the basis of quantitative data alone. Unfortunately, we did not
systematically gather materials on other aspects of the subject.

TABLE 4.9

*Comparison of Initial Attitudes Toward the Revolution of Members of
Political Exile Organizations and Members of Nonpolitical
Exile Organizations*

Initial Attitude Toward the Revolution	Members of Political Exile Organizations (N = 30)	Members of Nonpolitical Exile Organizations (N = 28)
Less favorable	53%	86%
More favorable	47	14
Chi-square = 7.10	$p < .01$	

We can, however, suggest what patterns of behavior would have to be explored in order to achieve a fuller understanding of participation through time.

First, we must distinguish between the refugees' participation in anti-Castro activity while still in Cuba and such participation in exile. The distinction is important because some of those who were active on the island were not active in Miami. When refugees talk about why they left Cuba, some mention that they were once engaged in counterrevolutionary activities on the island, fell under suspicion or came to doubt the efficacy of such activities, and finally left. Once in exile, many of them ceased their anti-Castro activities. Some were occupied with jobs, family, or adjustment to their new circumstances; some could find no ready means for translating their feelings into a satisfactory mode of action; others were convinced that if activity in Cuba had little effect, activity in another land would have even less.

For example, one of our respondents, a 35-year-old former sales promotion supervisor with a high school education, told the following story:

After I had been taken prisoner twice, demoted in my job from supervisor to peon, and harassed in my house, they [Castro supporters] appeared with a loudspeaker in front of my home to insult us for being against Communism. . . . They informed me that my situation was delicate and that if they took me prisoner again at work I would never get out of jail. Nevertheless, today there are moments when it pains me not to have perished in the struggle against Fidel because I came [to the United States] in search of help to overthrow him and find myself powerless to do anything for the millions of enslaved prisoners of my country. I feel that they have been abandoned and disgraced and their miseries exploited just for purposes of anti-Communist propaganda.

This respondent reported that he had not participated in any exile organizations since coming to Miami. On the other hand, there were other Cubans who had not participated in anti-Castro organizations on the island but were recruited into activism once they were in the United States.

Of course, there were also anti-Castro participants in Cuba who continued their activities after leaving. Some were attracted to exile specifically because they thought that Miami was "where the action is." One such respondent, a high school graduate who worked as an accountant for the Cuban electric company, told of his participation in these words:

Because I was convinced from the very first moment that the [Castro] government was Communist, I was against it, and I co-operated in every way possible to bring about its downfall. I had to come to the United States in August 1959, when the first con-spiracy against Castro failed. I returned to Cuba as soon as pos-sible. . . . I waited for one more year, thinking that when the North American properties were nationalized the U. S. Government would step in to prevent this action. The moment came, and nothing hap-pened. That is why I came here [to Miami], stirred by the rumors that an invasion against Cuba was being organized.

Later this exile joined the Bay of Pigs expeditionary force, but owing to organizational problems at the time of the invasion, he never landed on the island. Finally, there were a number of "continuing nonparticipants"—refugees who did nothing to aid the counterrevolution while in Cuba and have done nothing now that they are in exile.

By combining the four patterns of participation and non-participation in anti-Castro activities with participation and nonparticipation in anti-Batista activities at an earlier date, we generate eight possible patterns of longitudinal participation, shown in Table 4.10. None of the eight patterns is completely illogical. That is, one can imagine circumstances and beliefs that might have led a Cuban into any one of them. With our data, however, we cannot estimate the relative frequencies of the several patterns. As indicated in the earlier discussion of con-tinuing participation, we suspect that patterns one and three are fairly common. There is also good reason to believe that patterns five and seven are well represented among the refu-gees. Those refugees who did not participate in the fight against Batista, but who fought to overthrow Castro's government after

TABLE 4.10

Possible Patterns of Refugee Participation and Nonparticipation
in Anti-Batista and Anti-Castro Activities

Pattern Number	Participated in Anti-Batista Activity in 1958 and/or 1959	Participated in Anti-Castro Activity Before Leaving Cuba	Participated in Anti-Castro Activity After Arriving in U.S.
One	Yes	Yes	Yes
Two	Yes	Yes	No
Three	Yes	No	Yes
Four	Yes	No	No
Five	No	Yes	Yes
Six	No	Yes	No
Seven	No	No	Yes
Eight	No	No	No

he came to power, figured prominently in the Bay of Pigs adventure. Additionally, political and personal meanings attach to each of the other patterns. We have already noted that programs of internal security in Cuba crushed the counterrevolutionary activities and the hopes of many who had originally opposed Batista and later came to oppose Castro. As exiles, some of these counterrevolutionaries withdrew from political activity and involvement, feeling that nothing meaningful could be accomplished from Miami (in our schematization, such refugees fall into pattern two). They are probably among the most bitter and disillusioned members of the exile community.

We could speculate on the importance of other patterns, but enough has been said to indicate the kinds of questions with which any fuller discussion of sequences of political action would have to deal. Longitudinal questions of all kinds are central to an understanding of the revolution, and although we do not have sufficient data to examine political participation through time, we can shed some light on related issues. Specifically, we can detail the changing demographic and attitudinal composition of the outflow of refugees and the impact of events on that outflow. We turn our attention to these problems in the chapter that follows.

V

The Exodus

What began as a trickle of Cuban refugees into the United States in 1959 was, by the middle of 1962, a small flood. Just prior to the missile crisis of October, as many as 3,000 Cubans a week were arriving in Miami. (During the crisis, air service from Cuba to the United States was shut down, not to reopen for more than three years.) The increase through time in the flow of exiles is suggested by the data presented in Figure 5.1. Because we have data only for employable refugees who registered at the Refugee Center, the quarterly totals given in the figure greatly underrepresent the number of Cubans entering during any given quarter. However, the relative increases from quarter to quarter suggest the pattern of growth of the total influx. A rough estimate of the number of Cubans entering the United States in any given calendar quarter can be made by multiplying the number of employable refugees entering that quarter by four.[1]

The great increase in the quarterly totals of refugees undoubtedly reflects increasing dissatisfaction within the Cuban population as the revolution became more pervasive and radical. As new revolutionary programs were introduced and as existing

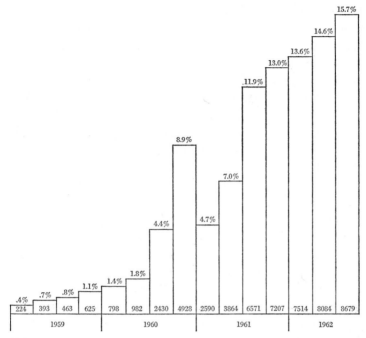

Figure 5.1. Number and percentage of all employable refugees entering the United States between January 1959 and September 1962, by quarters (N = 55,352)

programs gathered momentum, not only were more and more Cubans affected, but they were affected more profoundly—economically, socially, and politically. Many, of course, were affected in ways that were experienced as positive. But others experienced revolutionary reforms as unjust, threatening, and vindictive. We will treat this theme in some detail in the following chapter. At the moment, we wish only to emphasize the very strong association between the radicalization of the revolution and the increasing number of Cubans leaving their homeland.

One fact is important for placing the exodus in perspective.

why did Castro Let them leave

In the early months of the revolution there was no shortage of transportation from Cuba to the United States. Pan American World Airways alone had over 12,000 seats available each month for the trip from Havana to Miami. Furthermore, the necessary exit and entry papers were not difficult to secure. Thus, during 1959 and much of 1960 the flow of refugees was not significantly curtailed by lack of transportation or by political constraints. However, from the beginning of 1961 (the time of the break in diplomatic relations) to late October 1962 (the time of the missile crisis), fewer seats were available. Stringent exit and financial regulations further complicated emigration during this period, and it seems safe to assume that perhaps double the number of Cubans that left after January 1961 would have left had they been able to make the necessary arrangements.

Notable in the outflow of refugees, in addition to the increase in numbers, is the changing occupational "mix" through time. Occupations that are strongly represented among the refugees in some calendar quarters are less well represented in others. The differences can be seen in Figures 5.2, 5.3, and 5.4, where the variation within each occupation is plotted as a function of time and deviation from expected contribution. The metric on the vertical axis is the ratio of actual contribution to expected contribution. For example, since lawyers and judges constitute only 3 per cent of all refugees but 8 per cent of those who entered in the first quarter of 1959, the ratio of actual to expected contribution for this occupation in the first quarter is 8/3 or 2.7.

Our efforts to link overall changes in the occupational mix of the refugees to a chronology of events in Cuba were not successful. The emigration process and the occupational flow were too complex to allow us to make a cohesive set of relational statements of the form "When event X occurred in Cuba, persons of type Y left." Nevertheless, the data in Figures 5.2, 5.3, and 5.4 tend to substantiate the following limited propositions:

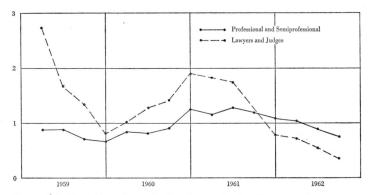

Figure 5.2. Variation through time in professional occupations among incoming refugees

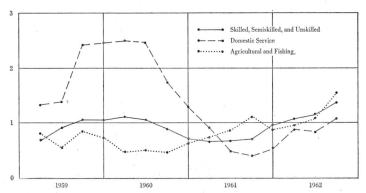

Figure 5.3. Variation through time in blue-collar, domestic service, and agricultural and fishing occupations among incoming refugees

1. The emigration of persons in occupations classified as professional and semiprofessional, managerial and executive, clerical and sales, and skilled, semiskilled, and unskilled was fairly constant through time. (In none of these groups did the ratio of actual to expected emigration fall outside the interval .5 to 1.5.)

2. The two peak periods of lawyer and judge emigration

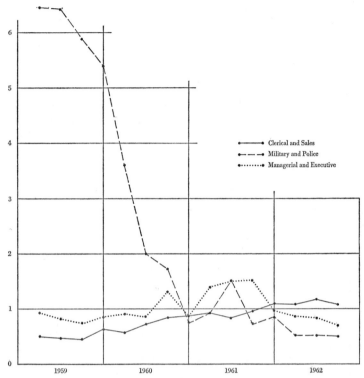

Figure 5.4. Variation through time in white-collar and military occupations among incoming refugees

followed the Castro takeover in 1959 and the promulgation of the far-reaching Urban Reform Law in the last quarter of 1960. These are events we might expect to have alienated large numbers of lawyers from the regime.

3. The major outflow of military and police occurred during 1959 and early 1960, as was to be expected.

4. The overrepresentation of domestic service occupations in the last half of 1959 and the first half of 1960 probably reflects the fact that during this period many wealthy families left as complete households, bringing their servants with them.[2]

Our inability to link specific revolutionary events to the changing occupational mix of the refugees does not mean that such events had no impact on the exodus. We have evidence of the importance of particular events in individual decisions to leave. For example, approximately 10 per cent of those in our survey sample said that the Bay of Pigs invasion was a factor in their decision to come to the United States. For some, the failure of the invasion demonstrated that Castro had consolidated his power, and nothing more could be done. Typical are the remarks of a 24-year-old high school graduate who had worked on a newspaper in Havana:

I decided to leave Cuba because the absurd failure of the invasion at Playa Girón [Bay of Pigs] showed me that the situation in Cuba had reached the point where the Communist domination of my country would last for at least two more years. Time has proved me right, and today I would say the same thing—that the Red domination will last perhaps another two years, until 1965. After I got out of prison—for in those days I was arrested along with thousands and thousands of Cubans—I made the irrevocable decision to leave Cuba.

For others, the primary importance of the invasion was neither its "absurdity" nor its failure, but rather the tightening of internal security that accompanied it. Among the thousands of Cubans arrested at the time of the invasion because they were suspected of being counterrevolutionaries, there were many for whom politics and political participation were relatively unimportant, and who—from their own point of view—had done nothing to warrant the treatment they received. One respondent, a 37-year-old office worker with a primary school education who had not actively opposed either Batista or Castro, said, "After the landing at Playa Girón, when they [the security forces] arrested me and all of my family just because we were Catholics, I realized that there was no security for any kind of man. I decided to leave."

Among other events respondents cited as important in crystal-

izing their decisions to leave were the forced resignation of
President Urrutia in 1959 and the trial and imprisonment of
Major Huber Matos later in the same year. Thus there is no
doubt that some refugees left Cuba in response to revolutionary
events of historical importance, but the outflows following such
events were not massive enough or socially homogeneous enough
to enable us to classify the Cubans involved as distinct sub-
groups.

Returning now to the overall characteristics of the Cuban
exodus, we note two important trends in addition to the increase in numbers and the changes in occupational mix. Semi-
annual data for the employable refugees entering during 1961
and 1962 indicate that each successive group was younger and
less well educated than the preceding group (see Table 5.1).[3]

An important question arises concerning the data in Table
5.1. Are the trends in age and education of the exiles due to the
changing occupational composition of the outflow, or are the
same trends to be found within occupations? To put the question more formally: If we hold occupation constant, do education and age still vary through time? In a previously published
article[4] we addressed ourselves to this question, and we can
summarize the results of our analysis as follows: The age trend
reported in Table 5.1 is accounted for by the change through

TABLE 5.1

Average Age and Education of Employable Refugees Entering the
United States in Each Half-Year Period from January 1961 to
December 1962

Period of Entry	Average Age	Average Number of Years of Education
1961		
January–June	42.4 (N = 113)	11.4 (N = 108)
July–December	41.2 (N = 232)	10.6 (N = 233)
1962		
January–June	40.5 (N = 270)	9.8 (N = 269)
July–December	37.8 (N = 265)	8.2 (N = 263)

time in the occupational mix. The occupational groups in which the average age is lowest contributed relatively more to the later stages of the exodus, while the occupational groups in which the average age is highest, such as the professionals, semi-professionals, managers, and executives, contributed relatively more to the early stages of the large-scale emigration that began at the end of 1960.

With respect to education, however, the situation is different. Within both the professional and semiprofessional group and the clerical and sales group there is a statistically significant educational trend during 1961 and 1962. That is, in each successive half year, the average educational level within these groups was lower than in the preceding half year. The same trend is also found in most of the other occupational groups, although statistical significance is not reached. This means that the rather sharp drop in educational level shown in Table 5.1 has two sources. First, the occupational mix changed through time in ways that decreased the relative representation of occupational groups with higher average education, such as the professionals and the managers. Second, within most occupational groups there was a lowering of average educational level through time. Although the educational differences within occupational groups were not dramatic, they suggest that a meaningful shift took place in status type within such groups—particularly in the type of professional, semiprofessional, and white-collar person leaving Cuba. The university professor was replaced by the grade school teacher, and the corporate sales manager by the retail clerk. Although we are still dealing only with trends, one point should be clear from this discussion: The drop in educational level in the exile population over time, taken together with the changes in occupational mix, suggests that by 1962 a considerable proportion of the refugees were neither rich, well-educated, occupationally advantaged, nor in any sense members of the pre-Castro "establishment."

In earlier chapters we have developed at length the idea that

for certain refugees self-imposed exile came only after an agonizing process of disillusionment and disaffection. We have seen
that many exiles once had very favorable attitudes toward the
revolution, and that a smaller, overlapping group participated
in the struggle to overthrow Batista. Returning now to the analysis of those members of our survey sample who participated
in or were very favorable toward the revolution, we can ask
how they differ from the less favorable and the nonparticipants
with respect to date of departure from Cuba. Briefly, we expect
both a favorable initial attitude toward the revolution and participation in the struggle against Batista to be strongly related
to late departure from the island. The reasoning is straightfor-
ward. Both the strong supporters and the participants had great
personal and psychological investments in the revolution. Such
investments kept them from early disaffection and departure in
at least four ways. First, as known supporters of the revolutionary cause they were undoubtedly less subject to social pressure,
harassment, and occupational dislocation during the first year
or two of the Castro regime than those who had been neutral or
pro-Batista. Second, they were ideologically better prepared
than others who subsequently left Cuba to accept the revolution's early programs and measures as necessary or even desirable. Third, even when the revolutionary government went
beyond what these early supporters and participants considered
proper methods and goals of social change, they were more
willing than others to excuse and justify such excesses as inevita-
ble under the circumstances. Fourth, when they finally began
to perceive the revolution as illegitimate and personally threatening, they required more than an average amount of time to
reconcile this perception with their earlier ideas, and to justify
both their initial support of the revolution and their subsequent
disaffection. In short, it took them longer to make up their
minds to leave.[5]

The posited relationship between time of decision to leave
and initial attitude toward the revolution is strongly supported
by the data in Table 5.2.[6] As we move from those who were

71

TABLE 5.2

*Time of Decision to Leave Cuba as Related to Initial Attitude
Toward the Revolution*

Time of Decision	Least Favorable (N = 31)	More Favorable (N = 91)	Most Favorable (N = 63)
1959 or 1960	61%	41%	25%
1961 or 1962	39	59	75
Chi-square = 11.5		$p < .01$	

initially least favorable toward the revolution to those who were
initially most favorable, we find that an increasing percentage
of refugees made the decision to leave after the beginning of
1961.

A similar pattern is found when we use data on participation
in the struggle against Batista. As Table 5.3 shows, participants
were much more likely than nonparticipants to have made up
their minds to leave after the beginning of 1961.

Because of the very strong relationship between favorable
initial attitude toward the revolution and participation in the
struggle against Batista, we suspected that the relationship reported in Table 5.3 might be nothing more than a restatement
of the relationship shown in Table 5.2. In other words, taking
participation into account might not increase our ability to account for the time of decision. To determine whether the participants' tendencies toward later departure decisions were
solely a result of their more favorable attitudes or also a result
of their participation, we examined each of the three attitudinal

TABLE 5.3

*Time of Decision to Leave Cuba as Related to Participation
in Anti-Batista Activity*

Time of Decision	Did Not Participate (N = 124)	Participated (N = 61)
1959 or 1960	46%	25%
1961 or 1962	54	75
Chi-square = 7.86	$p < .01$	

groups in Table 5.2 independently with respect to the relationship between participation and time of decision. More formally, we held initial attitude toward the revolution constant while running participation against time of decision.

It may be remembered from Chapter IV (Table 4.3) that in the group of refugees we designated as initially *least* favorable toward the revolution there were no participants at all. Thus we can drop this group from the analysis, because participation could not possibly have affected their time of decision. Turning to the group that was initially *most* favorable toward the revolution, we find that those who participated do not differ with respect to time of decision from those who did not participate (see Table 5.4). Although the subsamples are small, it is clear that the participation-nonparticipation dichotomy does not help us to explain the time of decision among those who were initially most favorable.

In the middle attitudinal group—those designated as *more favorable* —we find that there *is* a relationship between participation and late decision (see Table 5.5).

To recapitulate, those in our survey sample who were initially *least* favorable toward the revolution did not participate at all in the struggle against Batista, and their time of decision to leave Cuba must be explained in terms of some combination of initial attitudes and other factors. On the other hand, a substantial majority of those who were initially *most* favorable toward the revolution were active against Batista, but the time of

TABLE 5.4

Time of Decision to Leave Cuba as Related to Participation in Anti-Batista Activity Among Those Initially Most Favorable Toward the Revolution

Time of Decision	Did Not Participate (N = 24)	Participated (N = 39)
1959 or 1960	25%	26%
1961 or 1962	75	74

TABLE 5.5

Time of Decision to Leave Cuba as Related to Participation in
Anti-Batista Activity Among Those Initially More
Favorable Toward the Revolution

Time of Decision	Did Not Participate (N =69)	Participated (N = 22)
1959 or 1960	46%	23%
1961 or 1962	54	77
Chi-square = 3.87		$p < .02$

their decision to leave is independent of their participation in
the anti-Batista movement. Finally, the *more* favorable—those
with "lukewarm" attitudes toward the revolution—did not participate as fully as the most favorable group, but in this case
the participants tended to leave later than the nonparticipants.
From a behavioral point of view, the latter two patterns make
sense. Those who were initially most favorable toward the revolution were positively enough disposed toward the Castro government during the first years that their having participated in
the struggle against Batista did not add to their relatively high
levels of psychological engagement. Among those who were
initially less favorable, however, participation acted as an intervening variable, "immunizing" them against early disaffection from the Castro regime; thus they reached the decision to
leave later than they would have on the basis of their initial
attitudes alone. In this regard, it should be noted that approximately three of every four of the "lukewarm" refugees who had
participated did not reach the decision to leave until 1961 or
1962. This is almost exactly the proportion of those who decided late among both participants and nonparticipants in the
group that was initially most favorable.

We have now completed, in as much detail as the data allow,
our discussion of the demography, attitudes, participation, and
outflow of the refugees. We have a rather clear idea of who the
refugees are, how they differ from the home population, what

their political beliefs are, how they were initially linked to the revolution, and how the exodus has changed through time. All of this information brings us somewhat closer to an understanding of why they left, particularly when we can infer certain types of refugee experiences and motivations previous to exile from certain patterns of demography and participation. Such inferences, however, can lead to only partial explanations at best, and are dangerous if pushed too far. A proper understanding of why the refugees left must be sought in individual life histories, not in patterns of demography, attitudes, and participation. As emphasized throughout the previous chapters, Cubans left their homeland when they came to perceive conditions under Castro as intolerable. The variables we have examined to this point enable us to suggest which sectors of the population were most likely to come to such perceptions and when they were likely to do so, but much is left unexplained. We need to know what kinds of experiences, what kinds of reforms, events, behavior, and pressures were in fact perceived as intolerable by the refugees. Most basically, we need to know how individual lives had to be affected in order to produce the emotions and decisions that led to self-imposed exile. It is to this question that we turn in the following chapter.

VI

The Decision to Leave

One of the most striking characteristics of the Cuban Revolution was its pervasiveness. It is difficult to imagine any adult Cuban, no matter how isolated or how well-placed, who was not affected in some important way by the actions of the Castro government during the early 1960's. If he was rich, secure, and privileged, the revolution threatened his wealth, security, and privilege. If he was poor, insecure, and underprivileged, the revolution promised him a better life. However, the leaders of the revolution did more than talk about changes to come: they organized, legislated, destroyed, built, coerced, taught, grabbed, and acted in a multitude of other ways to achieve their purposes. One could not hide from or ignore the revolution. No corner of the island was too remote and no sanctuary too well guarded to remain untouched by it. By 1961, the national literacy campaign had reached the remotest parts of the Sierra, and long before that the masses were swarming over what, a few months earlier, had been the most exclusive beach resorts of Havana and Varadero. A person living in Cuba during this period knew that he was in a revolution—which, of course, is not to say that he understood what was going on.

Because the revolution was so pervasive, its meanings for individuals were determined by direct rather than vicarious experiences. That is, Cubans did not judge the revolution on the basis of what they were told about the experiences of others. Of course they talked endlessly about the revolution to relatives, friends, and co-workers; and without doubt their own experiences and opinions were modified, reinterpreted, or reinforced by the experiences and opinions of others. But almost everyone had his own story to tell—a story about himself or his family: a business expropriated, a stint in the militia, months in the Sierra as a volunteer teacher, a son or brother in prison, a child in school for the first time, land either taken away or received, an income decimated by the urban reform laws, a meeting with a revolutionary leader. The magnitude and the meaning of the exodus can be understood only in this light. People go into self-imposed exile only when they have experienced the effects of changes in economic arrangements, social structure, or political order in extremely personal and negative ways. Individuals may be alerted or sensitized by experiences of those outside the immediate family circle, but the precipitating experiences are personal and proximate. The Cuban Revolution gave large sectors of the population occasion to have such experiences.

Our data underscore this point. In separate questions we asked the members of our survey sample why they first began to think about leaving Cuba and why they finally left. We urged them to be as specific as possible, detailing incidents and experiences. As part of our analysis of their responses, we identified the "object" of each experience—the person or group that had the experience the respondent cited as instrumental in his first thoughts of leaving or final decision to leave. Usually, the object was fairly easy to identify. For instance, when a respondent said he was threatened with arrest, the object of the experience was clearly the respondent himself. On the other hand, when a respondent said only that the regime was Communist and therefore denied civil liberties, the object of the experience was society as a whole. In this second example, had the respondent said that *he* had been denied his civil liberties by the Communist regime, the object of the experience would have been the respondent himself, just as in the first example. The key idea at this point is that a set of events that affects society as a whole can be as meaningful to an individual as an experience that is very direct and personal in its consequences. In the second example, if the respondent had said specifically that he became frightened for himself and for his family when he saw the regime denying civil rights, we would have classified this as another experience in which the object is the respondent himself—even though, in the strict sense, the respondent and his family had not yet been "injured" by direct denial of civil rights. In short, if a respondent made clear the way in which an event or incident affected himself or his family, we considered it a personal or proximate experience rather than something that happened only to "others."

The categories used in the coding of "objects" were: (1) the respondent himself, (2) a member of the respondent's family, (3) a friend or acquaintance of the respondent, (4) some public figure not classifiable as a friend or acquaintance, (5) some social group or sector such as a union, the Church, or the middle class, and (6) society in general. As can be seen, these categories form a rough ordering from objects closest to the respondent to objects that are relatively remote. In Table 6.1 we present the frequency distributions of objects mentioned by our respondents. (In this table, categories three through six have been combined into one category—"other person or group.") Because respondents cited multiple experiences, we have placed first and second response columns under each of the two questions. There were very few third responses; as a result, these have not been tabulated.

There are two interesting patterns evident in Table 6.1. First, as we move from initial response to second response in both questions, the number of citations of family and others increases

TABLE 6.1

Person or Group Having the Experiences that Led Respondents to
First Thoughts of Leaving and Final Decision to Leave Cuba

	First Thoughts of Leaving		Final Decision to Leave	
Person or Group Cited	First Response (N = 202)	Second Response (N = 116)	First Response (N = 183)	Second Response (N = 95)
Respondent himself	85%	76%	85%	68%
Member of respondent's family	6.5	12	11	22
Other person or group	8.5	12	4	10

and the number of citations of self decreases. This is to be expected because respondents who cite several incidents are likely to mention personal experiences first, and then move on to describe things that happened to their families or to others. Second, if we compare the patterns under the headings "First Response," we see that the respondents cited fewer family experiences and more experiences of others when asked about first thoughts of leaving than when asked about the final decision to leave. An identical pattern is found in the second responses to the two questions. That is, the family was cited less frequently when respondents were first thinking about leaving and more frequently when they decided to leave. Conversely, other persons or groups were cited more frequently with regard to first thoughts than with regard to final decisions, although the differences here are not great. Again, the patterns make sense, because we would expect more proximate objects to loom larger in a refugee's final decision to leave than in his first thoughts of leaving. As the final decision drew near, the experiences of the family became more important than the experiences of other persons or groups.

Having established the overwhelming importance of self and family in both first thoughts of leaving and final decision to leave, let us turn to an analysis of the *content* or the nature of the experiences cited. What sorts of things happened to the

refugees and their families as the revolution began to assume
the pervasiveness of which we spoke earlier? Each individual
has his own story to tell, of course, but there is sufficient repeti-
tion and patterning of experiences to allow us to group responses under seven general headings. We will illustrate and
explain each of the seven content categories with quotations
from the refugees themselves.

1. IMPRISONMENT. Approximately 15 per cent of the respondents said that at one time or another they had been imprisoned
by the Castro government.[1] In the majority of cases the imprisonment came at the time of the Bay of Pigs invasion, when
thousands of Cubans suspected of harboring counterrevolutionary sentiments were rounded up and held for a period varying
from a few hours to several months. As mentioned in Chapter V,
many of those imprisoned at that time felt they had been arbi-
trarily and unjustly arrested and accused. Typical was the response of a 42-year-old mechanic of limited education who had
owned his own automobile repair shop before leaving Cuba
early in 1962:

Having never been involved in politics, living always for my work,
being respected by everybody, considered always to be a hardwork-
ing man and a decent person without political motivations, I was
imprisoned on the 17th of April 1961, and from that time on I was
persecuted constantly.

Others assumed no such posture of injured innocence. They admitted to us that they had participated in counterrevolutionary
activities, were caught at such activities or fell under suspicion,
and were sent to jail. For such refugees, prison was not an
alienating experience in which the sentence was perceived as
undeserved or the conditions harsh. Instead, imprisonment
served to convince them that the time to leave was at hand—
lest the next arrest bring a sentence of 20 or 30 years.

2. THREAT OR FEAR OF IMPRISONMENT. Closely related to actual imprisonment was the threat or fear of going to jail. Most

of those who left because they feared jail were well aware of why
they were being sought by the authorities, and thus the theme of
unjust accusation was little in evidence. For example, a young
lawyer who had left Cuba in 1959 told the following story:

Because I was a conspirator against the Communist government
that was being established and had left the country on several occasions with the idea of interviewing various officials of the Rebel
Army who had gone into exile in order to better organize the anti-
Castro movement, they [Castro's agents] began investigating my
trips. Our fundamental aim was to launch an attack on the police in
front of the Jesús de Miramar Church. Knowing that they were
investigating the principal participants, I decided to leave Cuba
[before they could take me into custody].

Other refugees were less overtly counterrevolutionary, but
realized that their beliefs, behavior, or allegiances had brought
them under suspicion, and that their future was at best extremely insecure. A skilled worker with an eighth-grade education,
very upset by political indoctrination in the schools, failed in his
first attempts to leave. Although originally motivated to leave
for family reasons, his attempts brought him to the attention of
the police, and he became the object of an attempt at entrap-
ment. The fear of arrest reinforced his desire to get himself and
his family out of Cuba. Finally he fled in a small boat.

I have three children, two boys and one girl. They would not give
us a passport although I tried three times. I tried three times to take
them out in a small boat and I failed. I even bought a boat from a
lieutenant in the G-2 [Castro's secret service] who then waited outside to catch us. Fortunately, a friend of mine, who was a prisoner
in the Castillo San Severino, warned us, so that I was able to keep
from being caught until I finally built a boat and was able to escape
with my two sons.... I left my daughter and wife in Cuba because
I was tormented and could not think clearly.

3. HARASSMENT AND PERSECUTION—THE DISRUPTION OF
DAILY LIFE. Many of the refugees were deeply disturbed by the
intrusions of revolutionaries—both the official and the self-

appointed varieties—into the rhythms and relationships of daily life. This was particularly true when they perceived themselves as having minded their own business and not overtly acted against the interests of the revolution. For some, these intrusions took the form of searches, brief arrests, periods of questioning, and then release. They were not imprisoned, but they profoundly resented the surveillance and suspicion to which they were subjected. For others, the intrusions were less dramatic but no less real. One source of intrusion was the Committees for the Defense of the Revolution, formed in 1960 as an island-wide citizen's organization;* these were particularly disliked by those who fell under the suspicion of local committees.[2] A barber with only four years of schooling voiced a recurring complaint:

It was impossible for us to live, because the Communist committees watched us day and night. Because we refused to cooperate with them, we were called counterrevolutionaries, which made our lives impossible. I want my children to be educated in a democratic system, where they can live in tranquillity.

This sort of surveillance assumed a special intensity and potential because it was organized on a neighborhood basis. As such, it was unusually disruptive of well established patterns of social interaction and expectations. The administrator of a small airport mentioned that "the atmosphere became very uncomfortable for me because I am a Catholic and an anti-Communist. My neighbors, including some that I thought were my friends, were constantly watching me."

The revolution made its presence felt not only at home but also at work. A barely literate truck driver from a small city in Pinar del Río said that at work he had been "persecuted as if I were a criminal" because he was not in accord with the manner

---

* The *Comités de Defensa de la Revolución* are organized on a geographical basis, and in densely populated areas there is typically one committee for each residential block. Official statistics published in 1963 gave the total number of committees as 102,500 and the island-wide membership as 1,500,000.

in which the government took over the business where he
worked. Later, he continued, "they accused me of sabotage at
work, which wasn't true. But that's the way the Communists are.
They don't have a mother [they're bastards]." In the middle of
1961 he came to the United States in a small boat. Others, although not overtly accused, were subject to constant harassment. A middle-aged man who was a driver for the Department
of Public Works, and who admitted that he was not particularly
cooperative with the worker-revolutionaries, told the following
story:

I couldn't be at ease at work because every day the lowest and worst
of the workers, who were the Communists, would say to me, "You
are a *gusano* [worm] and as soon as something happens here we
are going to look for you in your house and take it away from you.
You are *muy zorro* [a very foxy fellow]." There wasn't a single
tranquil day at work.

4. HARASSMENT AND PERSECUTION—FAILURE TO INTEGRATE
INTO THE REVOLUTION. The experiences included in this category are of the same order as those in the preceding one. The
key difference is that in these cases the harassment and persecution suffered are specifically attributed to failure to integrate
into the revolution in the prescribed manner.[3] In order to understand the meaning of revolutionary integration, it is necessary to appreciate the demands made by the regime on the time
and energies of the ordinary citizen. In Cuba, particularly after
the first months of 1960, it became very difficult to stand aside
and not participate. The revolution so dominated both public
and private life that neutrality and withdrawal were hardly viable alternatives to declaring oneself either for or against the
revolution. Castro has stated this dilemma very forcefully:

In a revolutionary process, there are no neutrals; there are only
partisans of the revolution or enemies of it. In every great revolutionary process it has happened like this: in the French Revolution,
in the Russian Revolution, in our Revolution. I'm not speaking of
uprisings, but of processes in which great social changes take place,
great class struggles involving millions of persons.[4]

In effect, the authorities asked "Are you with us or against us?" If the answer was "With you," then the citizen was required to demonstrate his "withness" or integration through participation in revolutionary activities. Failure to do so was taken to indicate not just lethargy or lack of interest, but counterrevolutionary tendencies. The term *gusano* came to be used not only for those who were overtly trying to destroy the Castro government, but also for those who were standing idly by—not participating positively as a good revolutionary citizen should. The life of the non-participant or the non-integrated Cuban was not easy under this all-inclusive dichotomization of the population into revolutionaries and *gusanos*. One refugee who tried to remain outside the revolution while in Cuba said, in desperation, "Life there was impossible. You had to be with them, or they would drive you crazy." Another summed up his perception of the situation in the starkest terms: "Under that government you could not remain neutral. Either you were a Communist or a *gusano*."

Pressures to integrate into the revolution were almost always connected with the respondents' occupations or, at least, applied through their places of work. For some, particularly the professionals, the pressures took the form of a reorienting of work responsibilities. They were given, in effect, a new or at least modified set of job specifications. For example, a lawyer who had been a provincial judge said:

As a judge I used to handle only minor offenses, was not involved with the government, and was independent. But in 1961 the pressures started to mount to make the judges political accomplices; they said over the radio that we should go and cut cane and teach the illiterates, which I always refused to do. One day a circular arrived from the authorities pressuring us to write "Fatherland or Death" after our signatures and demanding that we give classes in Marxism. That same day I resigned and started to take out papers to come to the U.S.

Another professional, the manager of a private school, said that he was troubled right from the beginning of the Castro regime.

Beginning in January 1959, in my position as manager of a private school, I noticed the inclinations of the so-called school authorities to impose conditions on teaching. They imposed them first and checked later to see that they were being carried out, making suggestions as to how civic instruction should be given, how the children should behave, and whom they should admire as patriots—not forgetting, they said, that this is a revolution of true patriots. . . . I believe that a school should not be mixed up with politics, nor politics with school.

For others—predominantly those whose work had little political significance or potential—pressures did not usually involve the job itself but rather after-hours activities. A young bookkeeper who worked in the Ministry of Transport complained:

They forced me to join the militia, telling me that if I did not do so I would be left without work. I was forced to go out and cut cane, and if I didn't show up my absences were marked down—everything there was obligatory. These things were never done by any previous government.

5. LOSS OF JOB, POSSESSIONS, SOURCES OF INCOME. One of the most prevalent simplifications concerning the exodus is that it was in large part motivated by economic considerations. After being injured financially—the argument runs—whole sectors of Cuban society fled to the United States. There is, admittedly, an element of truth in this point of view. Some refugees responded in classic economic terms to our questions about reasons for leaving. For example, a rancher, caught in the agrarian reform, said, "I had a business jointly with my four brothers and my mother. . . . I left with my family in February of 1962, because life was becoming impossible after they had confiscated everything." A self-made small businessman, who had owned two laundries in Havana, sent his son to the United States in 1960. "After that, on November 4th, 1962, they stole my two businesses. What more did I have to wait for?" An elderly journalist who "lived only for my profession" said, "When the Castro government seized the *Diario de la Marina* and ended

publication of that newspaper, I was deprived of work and left Cuba."

But the striking thing about such statements is how infrequently they occur. Only about 11 per cent of the exiles mentioned experiences that could be classified under this heading. The low percentage of refugees mentioning economic deprivation or property loss as a factor is particularly striking, because in terms of their incomes, almost two-thirds of the members of our sample had in fact been hurt by the revolution. We asked the respondents how much money they had earned in 1958 and how much they had earned during their last 12 months in Cuba. From these two figures we calculated that under the revolutionary government, approximately 64 per cent of the refugees had lost income, 18 per cent had gained, and another 18 per cent had neither gained nor lost.[5]

With so many having lost income, why did so few cite economic reasons for leaving? There are three possible explanations. First, loss of income did not in all cases mean loss of purchasing power or decline in standard of living in revolutionary Cuba. As a result of the reduction of urban rents and provisions for free education and medical care, many salaried people found themselves just as well-off economically in the early 1960's as they had been under Batista, despite a cutback in wages. Second, of all possible reasons for leaving, economic motivations were probably the most difficult to admit. Some respondents undoubtedly wished to avoid giving the impression that they were "materialistic," which would have been conveyed by their saying that they left because they were not doing as well financially under Castro as they had done under Batista. To abandon La Patria for a "mess of pottage" is not particularly heroic. Finally—and we attach most importance to this explanation—it is possible that for the majority of refugees, economic deprivations (at least of the kind they suffered under Castro) were simply not highly salient among the reasons for leaving Cuba.[6] Economic deprivation, taken alone, has never been a good predictor of individual political behavior. At the very least, such deprivation must be seen in some larger context before it assumes political meaning. When deprivation was spoken of at all by the refugees in our study, it was usually placed in just such a social and political context. Because most salaried people were able to continue in their original jobs or were given substitute work, only such persons as landowners, landlords, and self-employed businessmen were hit hard by the economic reforms of the government. But even among the minority that was "wiped out" by the revolution, financial losses were perceived as only one facet of an upheaval that divested them of power, privilege, and all the perquisites of high social standing. Thus, as refugees, they usually do not single out economic injury for emphasis. This is understandable, for their perceptions of reality are not neatly divided into economic and noneconomic categories. The revolution destroyed them economically, socially, and politically, and they see themselves as refugees from everything the revolution stands for. They are, in Cuban slang, classic *siquitrillados*: those who have been totally broken by the revolutionary process.*

6. TOOK EXCEPTION TO GOVERNMENT ACTIVITIES THAT HAD A DIFFUSE AND GENERAL IMPACT (COMMUNISM NOT MENTIONED). Many refugees did not mention specific incidents or experiences when they told us about their decisions to leave. They spoke instead of the imposition of a social and political order that violated certain deeply felt values and made impossible the continuation of life-styles to which they were accustomed. They had

* Leslie Dewart defines a *siquitrillado* as "one who has a broken backbone. This colloquial expression emerged into general use in 1959 from the argot of cock-fighting to designate a person, specifically a non-batistiano, whose interests had been damaged by the social measures adopted by [the] revolution" (*Christianity and Revolution* [New York, 1963], p. 170). The Cuban usage is actually stronger than indicated by Dewart. Anyone who has seen a cockfight knows how thoroughly mangled the losing rooster is. The *siquitrillados* are those whom the revolution destroyed in analogous fashion. As we emphasized earlier, they constitute a minority of the adult refugees. The majority was affected in less dramatic if no less meaningful fashion.

had enough of the new society—a society they viewed not only as illegitimate and coercive, but also as un-Cuban.[7] An articulate accountant with a high school education spoke for many when he said:

My decision to leave was like that of thousands of Cubans. We were accustomed to a democratic way of life. We dedicated ourselves to family, work, and friends, and expressed our thoughts about all things freely. Then suddenly a brutal change came into our lives. Our democratic, religious, and cultural institutions were crushed overnight. There was complete disunity in the Cuban family—fathers against sons, brothers against brothers, childhood friends converted into enemies: in short, a series of occurrences befitting savages, not human beings.

Other respondents singled out specific aspects of the new socio-political order for detailed criticism. Very often a respondent's sensitivity to one or another type of government activity or program could be traced to work-connected values. Thus, a lawyer who said, "My hair stands on end when I think of the trials at the beginning of this hateful regime," also commented that what bothered him most was "the lack of security":

From the beginning of the dictatorship, intervention in the most private life of the citizens took place. They didn't respect the privacy of one's home; they would search private homes at any time of the night. After stealing many of the family's belongings, they would arrest those who protested this abuse.

A young, university-educated accountant who worked in a bank saw the Castro government presiding over the destruction of all the economic institutions he had learned to respect.

I saw that they had taken everything away from people who had been able to achieve something with honest work. They had confiscated businesses and thrown the owners out—people who, after 40 years of hard work, had been able to achieve something such as building a small house to live in and another one to rent so they could have security in their old age. This just couldn't be. How could they take away even the desire for self-improvement? This is a system in which not only freedom but aspirations are taken away.

7. TOOK EXCEPTION TO THE COMMUNISM OF THE REGIME.
Much in the manner of those who objected to the activities of
the government in general, some refugees stated specifically that
it was the Communism of the regime—and the consequences
that, in their view, proceed quite automatically from Communism—that led to their rejection of the Castro government.
Many of these respondents cited incidents that they said were
crucial in awakening them to what was happening on the island.
Such incidents were not portrayed as gravely injurious to the
refugee himself but rather as experiences that alerted him to the
fact that Communists were taking over or were already in power.
Although usually unspoken, a basic premise in such cases was
that the respondent—quite apart from developments under the
Castro government—could not possibly live under a Communist
system. He had only to be convinced that Communists were in
power to have sufficient reason to go into exile. A young man
who had worked as a cashier in the Havana Hilton told the following story:

In a meeting at the Hilton Hotel where I was working, the leaders
of the hotel staff were giving us the reasons why the hotel had been
taken over. These were 100 per cent untrue because all of the figures
that they gave out were false. I knew the true figures myself. When
I asked to speak and said that there were some mistakes in these
figures, they told me to be quiet, saying that later on they would
explain it to me. Later, they called me in and told me that the
changes [in the figures] were not my affair but were the affair of
the hotel bookkeeper, and that I shouldn't try to slow the triumphant
march of the Revolution. It was then that I became convinced that
this was just another dictatorship and, worst of all, a Communist
one.

For others, the Communism of the regime hit closer to home, in
that it was perceived as threatening basic religious and familial
values. A middle-aged white-collar worker made this point directly:

I decided to leave because I could not accept living under a Communist regime. I am Catholic, and Communism denies the existence

of God. I saw that little by little the Communists were tightening the noose around the Catholics, and I saw that education in the private schools was being dominated by the Communists. I knew that my family would be irrevocably destroyed if I remained in Cuba.

The regime's official embrace of Marxism-Leninism played a special role in the process of disaffection of many Cubans. For them, this was not just another twist or turn in the ideological history of Castroism. It was seen as a complete break with the past and with Cuban political traditions. When respondents cite Communism as instrumental in their decision to leave, this does not seem to be simply a catchall response for those who could think of nothing else to say. There existed in Cuba a very strong strain of anti-Communist feeling, resulting in part from the Cold War and in part from the unsavory collaboration between the pre-Castro Communist party (Partido Socialista Popular) and Batista. Even though the regime's self-identification as Marxist-Leninist was not accompanied by a radical change in behavior on the part of the revolutionary government, negative associations and expectations were triggered by the realization that the revolution had "gone Communist." Sprinkled throughout the responses to our questions concerning the decision to leave Cuba are suggestions that actions that might have been endurable if perpetrated by overzealous Fidelistas were absolutely unacceptable when seen as part of the systematic communizing of Cuba.

This completes our list of categories used in classifying responses to the questions concerning why refugees left Cuba. Approximately 85 per cent of all responses fit into one of the above categories, which—taken together—suggest the range of experiences that led to disillusionment and disaffection.

Table 6.2 gives the percentage distributions of primary responses to both the question concerning first thoughts about leaving and the question about the final decision to leave. The first seven categories in the table are those we have discussed

TABLE 6.2

Primary Experiences that Led Respondents to First Thoughts of
Leaving and Final Decision to Leave Cuba

Experience Cited	Percentage of Respondents	
	First Thoughts of Leaving (N = 202)	Final Decision to Leave (N = 183)
1. Imprisonment[a] ....10%[b]		8%
2. Threat or fear of imprisonment 4		12
3. Harassment and persecution— the disruption of daily life 6		10
4. Harassment and persecution—failure to integrate into the revolution 9		13
5. Loss of job, possessions, sources of income 7		6
6. Took exception to government activities that had a diffuse and general impact 29		20
7. Took exception to the Communism of the regime 19		17
8. Other experiences of self or family 7		10
9. Experiences of person(s) or group(s) other than self or family 8		4

[a] In this, as in all other categories, one cannot simply add the respondents who cite the experience with regard to first thoughts of leaving to those who cite the same experience with regard to the decision to leave in order to determine the total number of refugees who claim the experience in question. There is a great deal of overlap between the two groups. That is, many of those who cite prison in response to the first question also cite prison in response to the second. In some cases, such respondents are referring to separate experiences, a first arrest and a second arrest. In other cases, first thoughts and final decision resulted from the same experience. Earlier in the text, when we spoke of the approximately 15 per cent of the refugees who had been imprisoned (or cited imprisonment) this figure was calculated by counting the number of respondents who in *any* response to *either* question said that they had been in jail.

[b] These figures total less than 100 per cent because of rounding.

above, giving the distributions only for refugees who mentioned self or family as having had the experience cited. Category eight includes experiences of self or family not included in the first seven, and category nine contains all experiences—no matter what their content—of persons or groups other than the respondent and his family.[8]

Not too much importance should be assigned to specific differences in the percentages given within the columns of Table 6.2. For instance, we could have grouped categories three and four together, in which case the amount of "harassment and persecution" would be quite striking, particularly in the second column, where it would be the most frequently cited experience. What is most noteworthy about the data is the relative evenness of the distribution of experiences. The revolution touched individual lives in many ways, and this is reflected in the many paths to exile suggested in the table.

Having noted that the table shows a relatively even distribution of varieties of experience, we can continue our quantitative analysis by combining the data. There is a "natural break" in the coding scheme that allows us to combine categories. If we consider categories one through five together, we can see that all the experiences coded therein are what might be called *pragmatic*. That is, prison, fear of prison, harassment, persecution, and loss of job or property are all experiences that touch the daily round of life of an individual, experiences that inevitably affect his work, family, and leisure activities. He might fail to comprehend the significance of such experiences and excuse or even embrace those who are responsible, but there is no way to completely avoid such experiences. On the other hand, experiences of the kind we have included in categories six and seven are, in the abstract, avoidable. By this we mean that the events could happen without requiring most individuals to deal directly with their consequences. In short, the events do not lead automatically to the experiences. Rather, they lead to the experiences only if the individual has made society's business his own. A completely apolitical man can live out his years in an environment of work and family that admits of no larger sensibilities. As long as he is left alone, nothing that happens to society at large—to the political process or to "others"—is seen as relevant to his own round of life. The experiences in categories six and seven could happen only to persons with some consciousness of the possible relationships between things that were happening "out there" and their own values and ways of life. For lack of more exact terminology, we will call such experiences *ideological*, with full understanding that we do not necessarily

attribute any coherent political position to those who cite opposition to the general activities of the government or to the Communism of the regime.[9]

We should make clear at this point that we are differentiating
pragmatic and ideological types of *experiences,* not pragmatic
and ideological types of *individuals.* We certainly do not claim
that all those who cite pragmatic reasons for leaving are in-
capable of making the kinds of associations between self and
society that ideological reasons connote. Some may in fact be
unable to make such associations, but we have no data with
which to identify those who by personality and life-style are
what might be called "constitutional pragmatists." At most, we
can say only that at a given historical moment, certain individuals seem to have been affected more by pragmatic than by
ideological experiences. Additionally, we do not believe that
those who cite ideological reasons were unaffected by events of
a pragmatic sort. We distinguish between pragmatic and ideological experiences precisely because we want to trace the conditions under which the balance of cited reasons shifted, first as
thoughts of leaving matured into decisions to leave, and second
as the revolution developed and changed.

Following up this discussion, the first point to be noted is
that ideological experiences were relatively more important
when refugees first began to think about leaving than when they
made the decision to leave. Using the data in Table 6.2, and
combining categories one through five as pragmatic experiences
and six and seven as ideological experiences, we generate the
pattern shown in Table 6.3. In view of the themes developed
previously, it is not surprising to find that the relative importance of pragmatic experiences increases as we move from first
thoughts to final decisions. The kinds of experiences that led
Cubans to question their place in the new sociopolitical order
are not necessarily the same kinds of experiences that led them
to leave their homeland. To cite an extreme example, an individual who has been made uneasy by measures that limit freedom

TABLE 6.3

*The Relative Importance of Pragmatic and Ideological Experiences in
First Thoughts of Leaving and Final Decision to Leave Cuba*

| | Percentage of Respondents | |
Nature of the Primary Experience Cited	First Thoughts of Leaving (N = 171)	Final Decision to Leave (N = 158)
Pragmatic	44%	58%
Ideological	56	42
Chi-square = 6.20	$p < .02$	

of expression is more likely to go into exile after being arrested
than after further curbs on the public's right to dissent. This
does not mean that he *must* be arrested before deciding to leave,
but only that a pragmatic experience is likely to move him
farther along the path toward an irrevocable decision than
another ideological experience. Similarly, an individual who
has begun to think about leaving because he has lost his business or property is more likely to decide to leave when he is
threatened with arrest than when he sees the legal system being
changed in ways that violate his political values.

What we are saying is that from the time of first thoughts to
the time of final decision, there are four possible patterns of
experience, not all of which are equally probable. The individual who first began to think about leaving because of a pragmatic experience is likely to have left because of the same or
another pragmatic experience. It is less likely that a subsequent
ideological experience would have been sufficient to precipitate
exile. Similarly, an individual who first began to think about
leaving because of an ideological experience may leave under
the impact of another ideological experience, but it is possible
that only a pragmatic experience would be sufficiently motiva-
ting to cause him to abandon his homeland. This interpretation
is borne out by an analysis of refugees who cited one type of
experience as responsible for their first thoughts and the other
type of experience as responsible for their decision to leave.

Of those who said they had had pragmatic experiences at the time of their first thoughts of leaving, less than 25 per cent said that they subsequently left because of ideological experiences. On the other hand, of those who spoke of ideological experiences with regard to first thoughts, more than 40 per cent said that pragmatic experiences were central to their decision to leave.

With regard to the relationship of ideological and pragmatic experiences to the *time* of the decision to leave, two arguments might be made. First, as the revolution became more radical, and particularly with the regime's public embrace of Marxism-Leninism in 1961, ideological issues of the most basic sort became paramount: freedom of dissent as opposed to the muzzling of opposition, Communism as opposed to non-Communism, Soviet influence as opposed to American influence. In such an ideologically charged climate, it might be argued, the pressures to take sides, to declare one's political position, and to reconcile personal values with sociopolitical events were great enough to cause a relative *increase* in ideological experiences through time. On the other hand, it could be pointed out that ideological issues were raised in a basic way during the very first year of the Castro government—that the central question of reform versus radical revolution was being openly debated by the middle of 1959. This would suggest that those Cubans who left as a result of ideological experiences tended to leave during the earlier part of the exodus. For those who remained in Cuba during the first years of the Castro regime, those who were somewhat favorable toward the revolution in general and participated actively in it, pragmatic experiences would be needed in greater measure to break their remaining ties to the island. Thus we should find a relative *decrease* in ideological experiences through time.

Our data support the second interpretation rather than the first. As can be seen in Table 6.4, among those who left during 1959 and 1960, pragmatic and ideological experiences were

TABLE 6.4

The Relative Importance of Pragmatic and Ideological Experiences in the Final Decision to Leave as Related to the Time of the Decision

Nature of Primary Experience Cited	Percentage of Respondents	
	Respondents Who Decided in 1959 or 1960 (N = 57)	Respondents Who Decided in 1961 or Later (N = 90)
Pragmatic	49%	63%
Ideological	51	37
Chi-square = 2.89		$p < .10$

cited with equal frequency as central to the decision to leave. On the other hand, those who left during 1961 or later cited pragmatic experiences in the ratio of almost two to one over ideological experiences.

It should be noted that the relationship between date of decision to leave and the pragmatic-ideological dichotomy is not strong. Might it be simply a function of changes in the average age, education, or occupational mix through time? In the cases of age and occupation, the answer is No, for of the three variables only education is systematically related to reasons cited for leaving.[10] One would expect refugees with higher levels of education to cite ideological experiences more frequently than the less educated. The supporting argument is familiar: The capacity to make the semi-abstract associations between self and society on which ideological experiences depend is developed through both the school and nonschool environments to which the more educated are exposed. In short, an ideological frame of reference and an ideological style of expression are found more commonly among the educated than among the uneducated. Among our respondents, however, the argument is only partially supported by the data. Between those who have at least some secondary and those who have at least some university education, there are no differences with respect to the relative frequency with which ideological and pragmatic experiences are cited.[11] It is only when we combine these two groups and compare them with those who have only primary schooling that the expected relationship is found. Table 6.5 shows that most of those with primary schooling cite pragmatic experiences, while pragmatic and ideological experiences are cited with equal frequency in the more educated group.

TABLE 6.5

The Relative Importance of Pragmatic and Ideological Experiences in the Final Decision to Leave as Related to Level of Education

	Percentage of Respondents	
Nature of Primary Experience Cited	Respondents with Some Primary Education (N = 46)	Respondents with Some Secondary or University Education (N = 107)
Pragmatic	72%	50.5%
Ideological	28	49.5
Chi-square = 5.93	$p < .02$	

When we control for education and examine the relationship between cited reason for leaving and time of departure, we find that the pattern shown in Table 6.4 still holds in part. That is, we cannot explain the relationship between pragmatic experiences and later departure entirely on the basis of changes in the educational composition of the refugee flow. As might be expected, among all those who departed in 1961 or later, the group with the lowest educational level cited pragmatic experiences with greater frequency than the groups with more education; however, the difference is not statistically significant. Overall, time of decision is a better predictor of type of experience cited than is educational level.

There is one more set of comparisons that aids in clarifying the relationship between educational level and experience cited. In Chapter III we demonstrated that education is positively related to initial attitude toward the revolution: the higher the level of education, the greater the probability of more favorable initial attitudes. When we examine the relationship, within educational groups, of initial attitude toward the revolution and type of experience cited as central to the decision to leave, an illuminating pattern emerges. Although the subsamples in Table 6.6 are small, it is clear that only among the less educated is initial attitude toward the revolution related to the type of experience cited. Among these, however, the relationship is quite strong. Among those with secondary or university education, initial attitude toward the revolution makes no difference in the relative frequency with which ideological or pragmatic reasons for leaving are cited. Furthermore, persons with primary education who were initially favorable toward the revolution were as much disposed as the better educated to experience the events after 1959 within an ideological frame of reference. It would seem that many of them, having perceived the revolutionary movement positively before Castro came to power, were already "thinking ideologically." It is only among those with both a low level of education and initially less favorable attitudes toward the revolution that a majority cited pragmatic experiences. However, because the initially less favorable constitute a large majority among all those with only primary education, the proportion of pragmatic experiences shown for the less educated in Table 6.5 is high. This association between low level of education and pragmatic experiences should not be allowed to ob-

TABLE 6.6

The Relative Importance of Pragmatic and Ideological Experiences in the Final Decision to Leave, Among Educational Groups, as Related to Initial Attitude Toward the Revolution

Nature of Primary Experience Cited	Some Primary School[a]		Some Secondary School		Some University	
	Less Favorable (N = 33)	More Favorable (N = 13)	Less Favorable (N = 46)	More Favorable (N = 25)	Less Favorable (N = 18)	More Favorable (N = 18)
Pragmatic	82%	46%	50%	52%	50%	50%
Ideological ...	18	54	50	48	50	50

[a] Considering those with some primary school as forming a separate two-by-two table, chi-square $= 5.85$, p. $< .02$.

scure the fact that certain kinds of prerevolutionary experiences
(about which we can say little) leading to a positive initial attitude toward the revolution evidently sensitized the less educated
to ideological issues to much the same degree that schooling and
extra-educational experiences sensitized others.[12]

We have traced in some detail characteristics and relationships that involve the demography, the attitudes, the political
participation, and the experiences of the refugee community. It
is now time to attempt to view the process of self-imposed exile
as a whole. To what extent does the flight of Cubans call into
question the legitimacy of the Castro government, and how seriously, if at all, does the exodus undermine the effectiveness of
that regime? What have we learned about the general conditions
under which citizens become so alienated from the existing political order that they leave rather than make the adjustments
necessary to continued residence? We turn to these and related
questions in the concluding chapter.

VII

The Revolution and the Exiles

The data and analyses presented in the preceding chapters give us some idea of the social composition of the refugee community, and of the attitudes, experiences, and reasons for leaving Cuba both of individuals and of groups. More difficult to capture with survey data, and therefore less clear, are the larger meanings and consequences of the exodus considered as a whole. In this concluding chapter, we shall introduce some of these larger questions and indicate in a preliminary manner how they might be answered in the light of our data and in the light of other interpretations and evaluations of the revolutionary process. Specifically, we shall briefly consider four issues: (1) the meaning of disaffection and flight from Cuba, (2) the meaning of continued residence in Cuba and continuing participation in the revolution, (3) the legitimacy of the Castro regime, and (4) the exodus and the past, present, and future of the regime.

THE MEANING OF DISAFFECTION
AND FLIGHT FROM CUBA

Traditional Caribbean dictatorships have always led to the flight of political opponents. Trujillo's enemies plotted against

him in New York and San Juan, just as members of the 26th of
July Movement plotted against Batista in Mexico and Miami.
The history of Cuba, in fact, is particularly notable for its exile
movements. José Martí, the most celebrated of nineteenth-cen-
tury Cuban patriots, spent many years in the United States before finally returning to Cuba to die in the war against Spain.
Since that time, nearly every change of government in Cuba has
led to the exile of dozens if not hundreds of citizens who sought,
among other things, allies and resources with which to do battle
against the incumbent regime. But never in the history of the
island has there been an exodus of the magnitude of the flight
from Castroism. Earlier, exiles were numbered in the hundreds;
now they are numbered in the hundreds of thousands.

As we have tried to demonstrate in the preceding chapter, the
key to understanding the magnitude of the recent exodus lies
in an appreciation of the pervasiveness of the revolution. In
sharp contrast to traditional dictatorships, Castro's mobilization
regime left no social sector untouched.* The social structure,
economic life, and political institutions of the nation were at-
tacked with a thoroughness and at a pace that was unprecedented
not only in the history of Cuba, but also in the history of the
hemisphere. The period from 1959 to 1963 is properly termed
cataclysmic. The Mexican revolution brought much more death,
destruction, and disorganization in its early years, but the Cuban
revolution stands alone as the most far-reaching and rapidly
paced social transformation in the history of Latin America.
The exiles are the human precipitate of this unrelenting, com-
pact, and profound process of change. The Cuban revolution
was ruthless, but not in the sense that it involved organized bru-

* Exiles from the traditional dictatorships are usually *previously politicized* individuals who find their status as active opponents or "outs" untenable.
The pool from which such exiles may be drawn is always very small in terms
of the total population. On the other hand, refugees from Castroism come from
a much larger pool of potential exiles: all those affected negatively by the
frenetic activity of the regime. In the main, such persons are politicized, if at
all, *by the process of change itself;* they do not necessarily belong to the rather
narrow prerevolutionary political stratum.

tality and extermination. Those individuals who were hurt by revolutionary programs, cut adrift by institutional changes, saddened by the passing of the familiar order, or angered by the Marxism of the regime were rudely shouldered aside. Those who were willing and able to adjust and adapt themselves to the requirements of the new order were allowed to do so; those who would or could not were treated harshly. Uncertainty, suspicion, and considerable organizational chaos were the natural corollaries of the Castroite revolutionary style. Thus, the style of change reinforced the scope of change to create conditions perceived as unbearable or potentially unbearable by hundreds of thousands of citizens.

Although indispensable to our understanding, the pervasiveness of the revolution and its impact on individuals are not sufficient to explain the magnitude of the exodus. As emphasized by a number of writers, self-imposed political exile arises from the confluence of four phenomena: First, an individual must come to perceive his conditions of life as intolerable or about to become so. Second, he must attribute the shift from tolerable to intolerable conditions to the incumbent regime. Third, he must be able to conceive of an alternative place of residence and a means for getting there. Fourth, such an alternative must actually exist.[1] The perception of conditions as intolerable and the attribution of these conditions to the Castro regime have already been dealt with at length. What needs to be discussed now are the elements of the "structure of alternatives and opportunities."

Unquestionably, the admission of disaffected Cubans to the United States without immigration quotas or restrictions has been fundamental to the exodus. Castro, taking an extreme position, has said:

If before the Revolution the United States had permitted free entrance of Cuban citizens, without restrictions, a much larger number would have gone then than the total of all those who have left since the Revolution or who will leave in the future. To what other underdeveloped country in this hemisphere has the United States offered its citizens an opportunity to immigrate freely? Any other Latin American country to which it made such an offer would empty out overnight.[2]

One need not subscribe to the Prime Minister's estimates of hypothetical past or future exoduses to appreciate that U.S. authorities have taken unusual steps to facilitate the entry of disaffected Cubans, even going so far as allowing the majority to enter without visas. No other potential exile group in the hemisphere has been so advantaged. If Castro's policies created the potential for a mass exodus, U.S. policies made the exodus possible.

It should also be understood that for many refugees the United States in general and Miami in particular were not terra incognita. Not only were there historic patterns of exile, emigration, and travel from Cuba to Florida, but as the refugee community mushroomed and as an atmosphere of "little Havana" grew in certain sections of Miami, a self-sustaining dynamic of refugee inflow was established. Exile is less forbidding when one has friends, relatives, and a community to go to. Of the members of our survey sample, 70 per cent said they had close friends who were already in the United States when they arrived, and 67 per cent said they had relatives here. Problems of language, employment, and social adjustment were mitigated by the size and social supportiveness of the Cuban community to which new exiles came.

None of what has just been said should be interpreted as denying that the refugees encountered serious psychological, social, and economic difficulties in the course of exile. Nor should it be understood to mean that we are retreating from our earlier position of maintaining that the vast majority of exiles were "pushed" from Cuba by the revolution rather than "pulled" to the United States by hope of gain or the attraction of the "American way." We wish only to emphasize the fact that the structure of alternatives and opportunities was more conducive to a large outflow in the Cuban case than in most other instances of self-imposed political exile in the twentieth century.

Finally, we should emphasize that few if any refugees are torn by divided or ambivalent political loyalties. Those who at one time were strong supporters of the revolution had become fully disillusioned with the Castro government by the time of their decision to leave. As we noted at the beginning of Chapter III, our respondents were unanimous in their rejection of Castro, the revolutionary government, and its programs. Furthermore, most projected their own evaluations of Castroism onto the Cuban public in general. Thus, there is not even a suggestion in our data that the refugees consider themselves disloyal. In their view it is Castro and the Communists who have betrayed Cuba, who are disloyal. The typical refugee affirms a "higher loyalty" to Cuba, to *la patria*. He may deeply miss his friends and relatives in Cuba and the way of life his homeland represents or used to represent; but he does not, as a rule, question the correctness of his decision to leave. He is in exile from the government in power; he is in exile from *Cuba* only insofar as the Cuba he knew and loved has in his view been betrayed and despoiled by Castro. It would be a mistake to think of the exiles as alienated from their homeland in the sense that we think of certain youths, minorities, or intellectuals as alienated in other countries. *What Castro has done to Cuba* is at the center of exile attention. And precisely because it is perceived as having been "done to" Cuba, because it is thought of as something foreign, unnatural, and anti-Cuban, it can—in the refugee vision of the future—be undone.

THE MEANING OF CONTINUED RESIDENCE IN CUBA

Throughout this study we have focussed on reasons for leaving Cuba. Yet an understanding of self-imposed political exile demands an understanding of non-exile as well, for the latter is not simply the mirror image of the former. That is, for every disaffected lawyer, doctor, or businessman in exile we could find several prerevolutionary lawyers, doctors, or businessmen still in Cuba, perhaps disaffected, perhaps not, but nevertheless still on the island. For every refugee who was imprisoned, stripped of his livelihood, or harassed by the new militants, there are other Cubans who had similar experiences yet did not attempt to leave. For every Cuban who in 1959 welcomed Castro into Havana as the liberator of Cuba but now plots his overthrow from Miami, there are other Cubans who once celebrated Castro's triumph, have since become thoroughly disillusioned, and yet continue to live and work in Cuba. And, of course, there are hundreds of thousands if not millions of Cubans to whom the revolution has brought increased opportunities and psychological and material benefits, and for whom the very idea of leaving the new Cuba is anathema.

For a number of reasons we have not been able to do a study of non-exiles.[3] We can, however, distinguish among three types of Cubans who are still on the island, and we can say a few words about each group. First, there are those who would leave if they possibly could. They are so disaffected from the regime or so closely tied to persons already in the United States that they are literally waiting in line to leave the island. We can call this group the "unwilling non-exiles," for only the barriers of water, lack of transportation, politics, and the bureaucracy keep them in Cuba. It is impossible to estimate precisely the size of this group, but since the Varadero airlift began in December of 1965, approximately 3,700 Cubans have been flying to Miami each month. Estimates of the total number expected to leave—if the airlift continues—cluster around 250,000.[4] Because men of draft age and persons with certain needed skills are not permitted to leave, this estimate, although the best we have, probably underrepresents the total number of unwilling non-exiles in Cuba at the end of 1965.[5]

A second identifiable group of non-exiles are those who see themselves as having benefited from the revolution, or at least as having benefited more than they have been hurt. The members of this group may well constitute a majority of the Cubans still on the island. Such individuals are not motivated to leave. It is difficult to establish boundaries for this group, but it certainly includes a majority of the rural masses and the youth, and large numbers of the new bureaucratic, party, and managerial elites, no matter what their ages or social origins. It should be noted that this group is delimited on the basis of self-perceptions rather than objective criteria. The group is defined as all those who perceive the revolution as having been to their benefit, even though an outside observer might question the objective bases of such perceptions.

This second group contains many individuals who by the criteria used in previous chapters should have been prime recruits for exile. It includes former landowners stripped of their holdings, businessmen who had their enterprises nationalized, workers and others who have been harassed by the new militants, anti-Communists who are no more Marxist-Leninist today than they were seven years ago, and others who would claim that civil liberties and personal freedom have diminished under Castro. Yet for one reason or another, such experiences and attitudes have not led these individuals to a view of the revolution in which negative elements overbalance positive ones. Personality characteristics are involved, for some persons are clearly better able to tolerate deprivation, negative experiences, personal insecurity, and change than are others. Furthermore, differing value hierarchies help to explain why revolutionary programs, perceived as intolerable by some, are seen as at least partially necessary and thus not wholly negative by others. Also relevant is the fact that many of those hurt in some fashion by the revolutionary process were later able to incorporate themselves or be incorporated into new and often exciting social roles. After an initial period of dislocation and tribulation they were swept into the main current of revolutionary enthusiasm and change; they themselves became activists rather than persons acted upon (often such people had a rather high level of education or technical expertise). For such individuals, the psychological and social rewards gained in the course of serving the revolution soon came to outweigh whatever negative experiences they had suffered earlier. Where they had not initially belonged to the emerging order, now they were part of it, and as a consequence both personal and political insecurities diminished. Explosive social and political change of the kind generated by the Cuban revolution creates opportunities for new forms of participation even more rapidly than it destroys old forms. It is not surprising that some of those who were initially displaced by the reorganization of society found new opportunities and responsibilities that eased their integration into the revolutionary system and bound them to its future.

There is a third group of Cubans still on the island. Whereas the first group consists of those who would leave if they could, and the second group consists of those who have experienced the revolution more positively than negatively and are not motivated to leave, the third group is made up of those who have experienced the revolution more negatively than positively, yet still will not leave. The members of this group are of two general types. First, there are those who lack the experiential and perceptual bases needed to imagine alternatives to their present situation. One of the reasons there are so few exiles from the rural and lower-class sectors of Cuban society is that the overwhelming majority of those raised in such environments simply cannot imagine leaving the island or how they might go about getting out. We spoke earlier of the structure of alternatives and opportunities as a key element in the process of self-imposed exile. Everything we know about the relationship of social structure to information, cognitive styles, and resources tells us that those who are situated lowest in the social hierarchy are the most disadvantaged in terms of access to the skills and opportunities that allow dissatisfaction to be translated into self-imposed exile. Most of the peasantry and much of the urban lower class have never been presented with viable alternatives to continued residence in Cuba and continued participation in the revolution. Thus, we have two trends that reinforce each other. The more literate, urbanized, and wealthy Cubans were hit hardest and benefited least by the revolution, while at the same time they were the best equipped both in terms of experience and resources to imagine alternative styles of life and places of residence. Just the opposite was true of the less-privileged sectors. The revolution generated much less dissatisfaction in these sectors; deprivation, both real and relative, was less severe when it existed at all, and among the relatively few dissatisfied individuals the proportion of those who would or could seek relief through leaving Cuba was much smaller also.

The second type of dissatisfied Cuban who nevertheless does not seek to leave the island is distinguished from the first type by his perceptions of the possibility of self-imposed exile. Although he is aware of the structure of alternatives and opportunities, he does not choose or is not motivated to leave. The possible reasons for such an attitude are numerous. Foremost are the political apathy and inertia mentioned at the beginning of this study. As emphasized earlier, the scales are heavily weighted against leaving, even among those who are rather highly dissatisfied with the Castro regime. The easiest thing for them to do in most cases is remain where they are and "bear up." This is particularly true in a nation such as Cuba, which has known more than its share of political turmoil and dictatorship in the twentieth century. Although, as we have argued, the Castro regime is different from anything the island has previously experienced, it is certainly not unambiguously the most authoritarian government that has been known in Cuba, a country that has suffered under Machado and Batista. In any event, even in a revolutionary system individuals find ways to sequester themselves from the regime, escape from the more objectionable and obtrusive aspects of the mobilization society, or so organize their lives that their dissatisfaction becomes bearable. Although the regime attempts to insure that politics is of major concern to everyone, the ordinary citizen's ability to insulate himself from the political system is well known. In the Cuban case, ties of family, friendship, and common culture soften the hardships and mitigate the dissatisfactions, while the benevolent aspects of the new welfare state offset in part the material attractions of the United States.

It is not easy to estimate the size of this dissatisfied but un-motivated segment of the population. In a carefully done study of a systematic sample of Cuban workers conducted in 1962, Maurice Zeitlin classified approximately 70 per cent of his re-spondents as favorable toward the revolution, 12 per cent as indecisive, and 18 per cent as hostile.[6] He quotes one respondent as typical of a hostile worker: "I stay only because I have two daughters who will not leave—otherwise I'd go away. . . . No one bothers me; I just do not like it. Why? I can't say why. I guess I just prefer the old Cuba. . . ."[7] Unfortunately, there are no other available studies of attitudes toward the revolution done more recently than spring 1960, when little dissatisfaction with the regime was as yet manifest.[8] All we can say in the ab-sence of more complete data is that by the mid-1960's a sig-nificant minority of the Cuban population viewed the revolution more negatively than positively. Many if not most of these per-sons, however, were not and are not candidates for exile. They may be insufficiently disaffected to take the extreme step of leaving, they may not perceive the structure of possible alterna-tives in a fashion conducive to self-imposed exile, they may be tied to Cuba by an unbreakable network of familial and cultural relations, they may have made accommodations and arrange-ments that protect them from what they perceive to be the most unpleasant aspects of the new system, or their behavior may be best explained by some combination of these factors. In any event, it is important to realize that those already in exile and the unwilling non-exiles who are waiting to leave do not con-stitute the total of all those who are dissatisfied with the revolution. As we have seen, dissatisfaction with a political system, even with a revolutionary system as pervasive as the Cuban, does not automatically lead to self-imposed exile. There are many degrees and types of dissatisfaction, just as there are many responses to it; hundreds of thousands of Cubans who will never learn to love their new government are nevertheless learning to live with it.[9]

THE SUPPORT AND LEGITIMACY OF THE
CASTRO REGIME

In the light of the outpouring of exiles, one of the questions most frequently asked about Castro is "How much support does he really have?" When posed in this fashion, the question is unanswerable, because Castro's support, like that of any other political leader, varies through time and according to the issues involved. That is, in the aggregate he had less support in 1965 than in 1959, and his policies regarding education and public health have clearly always been more popular than his policies regarding such things as rationing and compulsory military service. The question of support becomes more open to analysis when we distinguish between two alternative but complementary ways of rephrasing it. First, we might ask how much satisfaction and dissatisfaction there are in Cuba, what the distribution of satisfaction-dissatisfaction is in terms of social and demographic variables, and what conditions or issues various segments of the population are satisfied or dissatisfied about. This is a classic "public opinion" question and one for which we have almost no Cuban data. We must again caution the reader against assuming that the population of exiles and potential exiles either exhausts or accurately reflects the population of dissatisfied persons; we would also caution him against assuming that the projections of exiles of levels of dissatisfaction on the island are an acceptable substitute for data.

A second way of rephrasing the question is to ask how legitimate the Castro regime is. Seymour Lipset has defined the concept of legitimacy as follows:

Legitimacy involves the capacity of the system to engender and maintain the belief that the existing political institutions are the most appropriate ones for the society. . . . Groups regard a political system as legitimate or illegitimate according to the way in which its values fit with theirs. . . . Legitimacy, in and of itself, may be associated with many forms of political organization, including oppressive ones.[10]

When defined in this fashion, the concept of legitimacy is freed from direct dependence on levels of citizen satisfaction. Even citizens who are deeply dissatisfied may nonetheless consider existing political institutions appropriate, and thus continue to participate in ways supportive of the system, either with an expectation that conditions will ultimately improve or with a resignation born of apathy and ignorance. Because it is a characteristic of the total system rather than a simple aggregation of individual attitudes, the legitimacy of a given set of political institutions cannot be inferred directly from data of the sort normally generated by public opinion polls. Similarly, predicting a crisis of legitimacy involves much more than a simple summing up of political dissatisfaction. It matters a great deal not only what groups or strata in a society reject the legitimacy of the institutional order, but also how willing and able they are to challenge the rule, rules, and institutions established or perpetuated by the incumbents.

In the context of the Cuban revolution, this view of legitimacy and crises of legitimacy leads us to consideration of a number of specific points. First, what inferences about the legitimacy of the regime may be drawn from the outflow and the characteristics of the refugees? As a starting point, we can assume that almost all the exiles view the Castro government as illegitimate. This is the meaning of their total rejection of Castro, Castroism, and Communism as inappropriate to the present or future of Cuba. However, one cannot assume that those who are dissatisfied yet do not choose to leave fully share the exiles' rejection of the new institutional and political order. If the concurrence of perceptions of the new order as both personally harmful and illegitimate is central to the decision to leave, then those who remain probably do not perceive the regime as illegitimate to the degree the exiles do. Furthermore, both the will and the ability of the dissatisfied to challenge the new order are severely limited by the nature of the new institutions. Because the regime does everything in its power to co-opt potential opposition, deprive dissidents of the opportunity to promulgate their views, and crush any who are actively engaged in efforts to overthrow it, overt challenges to its authority are rare indeed. Many of those who feel strongly that the new institutions are inappropriate are already off the island or in the process of leaving, and those who share such feelings and yet remain are not able to mount a serious threat to the incumbents.

Second, we should consider the other side of the legitimacy equation, the side not represented by the exiles. The strength of the Castro government is affected not only by the numbers and the political relevance of those who consider it illegitimate, but also by the numbers and the relevance of those who consider it "super-legitimate." The exiles represent a passionate minority who reject the new order, but there is another passionate minority that has embraced the new order and that works actively to ensure its survival and success. It is probable that this second passionate minority outnumbers the first, and it is undeniable that it is now much more strategically located. For every Cuban who has left, there is another and possibly two or three others who live and would die for the revolution. As a rule, these passionate revolutionaries tend to be young, of modest education, and of limited pre-Castro experience.[11] In a very real sense they are the children of the revolution, found in the Party, the military service, the schools, fields, and farms of Cuba. Led and tutored by an older, more experienced, but still youthful generation of revolutionaries, they constitute an impressive and increasingly important source of support for the new regime. Just as the revolution is the primary object of attention for the passionate minority who consider it illegitimate, so it is the primary object of attention for a second passionate minority—those who would die defending it. One cannot help but feel that the second group has for some time been of more consequence, both numerically and politically, for the legitimacy of the regime than the first.

A third consideration enters into the analysis of the legitimacy of the new order in Cuba: the centrality of Castro to the revolutionary process. We do not refer to his decision-making power, however great that may be, but rather to his symbolic and legitimating functions. Perhaps nowhere in the modern world has charismatic legitimation of a new institutional order been as profound and as critically important as in Cuba.[12] As much as Castro is despised by the exile community, he is just as profoundly beloved—and therefore invested with special powers—by his passionate followers. For one group he is Judas incarnate, for the other he is both David and Moses—giant slayer and liberator. Thus, the most important of the "existing political institutions" that vast numbers of Cubans believe to be "appropriate ones for the society" is Fidel Castro himself. Anyone who has seen Castro at work among the Cuban masses can appreciate a position frequently (though privately) expressed by many Cubans: *"No soy marxista, soy Fidelista"* (I'm not a Marxist, I'm a Fidelist).[13] Although Castro himself has worked to transfer some measure of the legitimating authority from his own person to the new institutions of the revolution, how successful he has been or will be remains to be seen. And until such transfer takes place to a substantial degree, all the strengths and weaknesses associated with basing legitimacy on charismatic authority will continue to characterize the Cuban situation. In the meantime, exile rejection of Castro should not be taken to indicate Cuban opinion in general. The fervor with which the exiles despise and reject Castro is equalled by the fervor with which many other Cubans embrace him.

THE EXODUS AND THE PAST, PRESENT, AND FUTURE
OF THE REGIME

In earlier chapters we emphasized that the Cuban revolution must be viewed in its several phases and in historical perspective if the outflow of exiles is to be understood. Among all the employable Cubans who entered the United States and registered with the Refugee Center during the first four years of the revolution, only 3 per cent entered in 1959, and less than 17 per cent entered in 1960. It was not until 1961 and especially during the first nine months of 1962 that the exiles began to pour in by the thousands each month. The latter two years, of course, were the critical transitional years from the relatively ambiguous early revolutionary period to the clearly defined Marxist-Leninist period. The year 1961 opened with the break in diplomatic relations between the United States and Cuba; 1962 closed, for purposes of our analysis, with the missile crisis of October. In the intervening months, the exile troops were defeated at the Bay of Pigs, the revolution was officially declared to be Socialist, Castro announced "I am a Marxist-Leninist," and Cuba was excluded from the Organization of American States. Although it can be argued in retrospect that the course the revolution was to take was apparent even in the latter part of 1959, the dramatic increase in the number of refugees from 1961 through October of 1962 suggests that for the majority of those who left during the first four years, the events and conditions of 1959 and 1960 were not perceived as intolerable, however bothersome and disturbing they might have been. It was not the Castro takeover but rather the radicalization of the revolution and the formal embrace of Marxism-Leninism that gave rise to the most critical tests of individual allegiance to the emerging order. As we have seen, tens of thousands of Cubans would have nothing to do with the new way of life.

The rejection of this new way of life was profoundly affected by prior experiences and by allegiance to the old way of life— or at least to certain aspects of the old way of life. *Comparisons* as well as *deprivations* are at the core of exile perceptions and motivations. The worker cited earlier who said, "No one bothers me, I just do not like it. Why? I can't say why. I guess I just prefer the old Cuba. . . ." spoke for many who had undergone what Eric Hoffer has called the ordeal of change.[14] During 1961 and 1962, not only were businesses, lands, jobs, and possessions lost, but familiar patterns of daily life were transformed, social relations were disrupted, and the established universe of political and economic discourse was overturned. It was, to say the least, a difficult period, not only for those individuals located at critical junctures in the pre-Castro web of social and economic relations, but also for those less privileged persons who were asked to trade familiarity for unfamiliarity, security however modest for insecurity however promising, or the comfortable pursuit of private matters for a less comfortable participatory role.[15] Those Cubans who were old enough to have a prerevolutionary model with which to compare the state of affairs in 1961 and 1962, and well-placed enough to be personally affected by the hardships and restrictions brought by the radicalization of the revolution, were doubly susceptible to the impact of the ordeal of change. For such individuals, comparisons and deprivations were closely related: the former gave rise to perceptions of the latter.

The centrality of the years 1961 and 1962 to the process of disaffection and exile has certain implications for the present and future of both the exodus and the revolutionary regime. It can be hypothesized that many of those leaving after the autumn of 1965 did so because of experiences they had had and attitudes they had formed several years earlier. We have no attitudinal data on the new exiles, but it is our impression that many if not most of them would have left much earlier had the flow of refugees not been choked off in October 1962. Now they come as the crest of an exodus that was dammed up very abruptly for political reasons. It is difficult to imagine that events from 1963 through 1965 served to disengage from the new order large numbers of Cubans who were not already partially disaffected and inclined to leave by the end of 1962. During the period after the missile crisis, previously ambivalent individuals may have decided definitely to leave, and the decisions of those determined to get out as quickly as possible may have been reinforced, but the Cuban who had managed to maintain some meaningful attachment to the regime during 1961 and 1962 was not very likely to have had that attachment ruptured by events that came later.

This interpretation is supported at least indirectly by the occupational data in Table 7.1. There it can be seen that the occupational profiles of refugees arriving in 1966 and 1967 are not greatly different from the profile of those who arrived in 1962. The one striking exception is that the percentage of pro-

TABLE 7.1

Occupational Comparison of Employable Refugees Arriving in 1962, 1966, and 1967

Occupation	1962[a] (N = 27,419)	1966[b] (N = 17,124)	1967[c] (N = 14,867)
Professional, semiprofessional, and managerial	31%	21%	18%
Clerical and sales	33	31.5	35.5
Skilled	17	22	26
Semiskilled and unskilled	8	11.5	8
Service	7	9	8.5
Agricultural and fishing	4	5	4

[a] Recalculated from 1959–1962 roster of all employable refugees (see Chapter Two).

[b] Covers the period from December 1, 1965, to December 31, 1966. Data are from Cuban Refugee Emergency Center, "Cuban Refugee Program, Consolidated Report on Overall Operation, Month of December, 1966" (January 1967).

[c] Covers the period from January 1, 1967, to December 1, 1967. Data are from Cuban Refugee Emergency Center, "Cuban Refugee Program, Consolidated Report on Overall Operation, Month of November, 1967" (December 1967).

fessionals and managers has declined while the percentage of
skilled workers has increased. However, as noted in Chapter
Five, tendencies of this sort were already apparent in the influx
of refugees that preceded the missile crisis. The occupational
profiles of those who came in the first two years of the airlift
suggest that there has been no important shift in the type of
Cuban who experiences conditions under Castro as intolerable.
In particular, those in semiskilled, unskilled, service, and agricultural occupations contributed only slightly more to the influx
in 1967 than they did in 1962; and in the aggregate, these occupations are still underrepresented in the refugee flow by a factor of about eight when compared to the general working population of Cuba.

To many critics, Cuban society may not look any more attractive in the middle and late 1960's than it did in 1961 and
1962. But it is clear that time lessens the personal impact of the
most difficult years of transition from capitalism to communism,
and even some deeply disaffected individuals who might have
left in late 1962 had they been able to had made their peace
with Castroism by the end of 1965. Furthermore, by the beginning of 1966 an entire generation of Cuban youth had grown
up under the revolutionary system. Knowing no other style of
life, not able to make the comparisons that trouble their elders,
and in general well treated—even privileged—under the new
regime, this generation and those that follow will be increasingly
unlikely to resort to exile as a solution to personal dissatisfaction. Like youth in both the Eastern and Western worlds, to the
extent that they come to be dissatisfied with the environments
in which they live, most will probably choose to work for change
from within or to "drop out," that is, to disengage themselves from the larger society—if that is possible—rather than
flee from the national territory. Dissatisfaction among certain
groups in Cuba will continue, of course, and new sectors will
come to view the revolutionary society as less than perfect. But
this does not mean that disaffection sufficient to lead to self-

imposed exile will result. Although bitter enemies of the revolution would like to think that coming generations of Cubans will
find the new order as intolerable as they themselves found it, history teaches otherwise.

In evaluating the overall significance of the exodus, it is important to realize that Castro and his lieutenants have always
displayed a certain ambivalence toward the migration—both en-
couraging it and discouraging it. What might be called the "pu-
rification" theme has tended to dominate both official rhetoric
and policy. The thrust of this argument is that the revolution is
better off without those who cannot or will not adjust and integrate. This point has been emphasized by Castro and others on
numerous occasions:

In this country, when we say to someone, "If you want to leave, we
aren't going to stop you; you are free to leave," this country doesn't
lose a citizen. Why? Because that citizen could never be considered
—from our revolutionary point of view, from our Marxist point of
view—a [true] citizen of this country.[16]

On the other hand, the regime has never been happy with two
other consequences of the exodus. First, there is the drain of
much-needed technical and professional personnel. Second,
there is the demonstration effect of the movement. The Cuban
leaders know, just as the general population knows, that the refugees do not come exclusively from the privileged sectors of the
old order. Almost every urban family in Cuba has a relative,
friend, or acquaintance either in exile or waiting to leave. Most
urban Cubans certainly realize that great numbers of persons
with life-styles similar to theirs have opted for exile. The regime
therefore considers it necessary to discredit the motives of those
who leave, to question their courage and patriotism, and to dep-
recate their manner of life in the United States. The attitude of
the regime is well summed up in the epithet *gusano* (worm),
applied by the revolutionaries to the exiles, and it is clearly conveyed by the following poem:

Witness for the Prosecution

Every day at a quarter to three,
She would enter the Dime Store cafeteria,
Place her elbows delicately
On the shiny counter of formica,
As though it were a precious piece of crystal,
Order her ice cream, vanilla,
An ice cold coca cola with a straw,
Syrup and a great big wedge of cake.
Unhurriedly she would consume it all
And descend from the revolving chair,
Like a Twentieth Century goddess.

This was every week day.
I never knew what she did on Saturday afternoons.
But at night she rode about
In her cousins' convertible,
Sat near the dance floor
In the most exclusive cabaret,
And drank rum with soda.
I used to watch her in the afternoon
From behind my dark-colored glasses.
Once I knew her name but forgot it later.
She worked in the office of a foreign concern,
Lived in a two-story house without a garden.
She had studied to be a teacher,
And then was probably about 23 years old.
I believe she left about 1961,
Although I couldn't prove it.
She never interested me personally.
(She did interest George, but I imagine
He's forgotten all about it by now.)
I liked to observe her, since she was
A symbol of the mechanical life
Of a certain social type
Who consumed an expensive snack
At a quarter to three every afternoon.

It would be hard for me to believe
That she is still here.

> Would she be likely to put up
> With voluntary work, queues, ration books,
> A possible shortage of chocolate cake?
> It may simply be a prejudice of mine,
> Some remnant of old frustrations,
> But people like her
> Are incapable of the slightest sacrifice.[17]

In his public pronouncements, Castro has expressed similar thoughts on many occasions. For instance, speaking to tens of thousands of Cubans in the Plaza of the Revolution on September 28, 1961, he said:

If some more want to go to Miami, let them go to Miami! Each time that a boatload of parasites leaves—whether for Spain or for Miami—the Republic comes out ahead. What do you lose, working men and women? What do you lose, men and women who live in slums, who live in shacks, who live in the poor sections of town? What do you lose when a parasite leaves? One less beefsteak eater, one less driver of a fancy car, one drinker less ... and if he has a good apartment, that apartment will go to a working family that has a lot of children.[18]

Despite what are perceived to be the negative aspects of the exodus, however, Castro has chosen to export most of his enemies rather than try to force or beguile them into the revolutionary system.[19] Although this policy has not been followed with perfect consistency over time, it has served to ease the transition to communism for all concerned. To argue in this fashion is not to say in some abstract fashion that the new society was or is good, just, or even needed. We are saying only that once the drive toward the great transformation was undertaken, the human costs were necessarily going to be high. It is not pleasant to imagine what measures might have been taken against those who are now refugees if exile had not been a viable alternative. Nothing we know about Fidel Castro or about major social revolutions leads us to imagine that the hundreds of thousands of disaffected Cubans now in exile would simply have been put to pasture if they had not been able to leave.[20] There is no reason to believe that such an unassimilable mass of citizens would have been allowed to stand in the way of the achievement of revolutionary goals as those goals were defined by Castro. Although those individuals intimately affected by the exodus will probably never be able to perceive it as one of the more humane solutions to the trauma of change in contemporary Cuba, it may well be so characterized when the history of the Cuban revolution is finally written.

Appendix A

CUBAN REFUGEE EMERGENCY CENTER
600 Biscayne Boulevard
Miami 32, Florida

Miami, March 18, 1963

DEAR SIR:

I am pleased to inform you that you have been selected as a member of a group of refugees who will be interviewed about their experiences in Cuba.

In order to facilitate your attendance at this interview, we have arranged four meetings which will take place on four different evenings at the Cuban Refugee Center, 600 Biscayne Boulevard, Miami. We ask that you choose the date that is most convenient, but that you do not come to more than one of these meetings.

The meetings will take place on the following evenings:
Monday, March 25, at 7:30 p.m.
Tuesday, March 26, at 7:30 p.m.
Wednesday, March 27, at 7:30 p.m.
Thursday, March 28, at 7:30 p.m.

ATTENTION: Please bring this letter to the meeting that you decide to attend because without it you cannot be admitted. Also, everyone will be paid $1.00 as reimbursement for round-trip expenses from his home to the Refugee Center.

DON'T FORGET: Attend one of these meetings and bring this letter with you.

We look forward to seeing you,
RICHARD BRODY
Project Director

CUBAN REFUGEE EMERGENCY CENTER
600 Biscayne Boulevard
Miami 32, Florida

Miami, el 18 de marzo de 1963

ESTIMADO SEÑOR:

Tengo a bien comunicarle que usted ha sido seleccionado para integrar un grupo de refugiados que serán entrevistados acerca de sus experiencias en Cuba.

A fin de facilitar su asistencia a esta entrevista, hemos organizado cuatro reuniones en cuatro noches diferentes a llevarse a cabo en el Centro de Refugiados Cubanos, 600 Biscayne Boulevard, Miami. Le solicitamos que escoja usted la fecha que le sea más conveniente, pero que no asista a más de una de estas reuniones.

Las reuniones tendrán lugar en las siguientes noches:

Lunes, 25 de marzo a las 7:30 p.m.

Martes, 26 de marzo a las 7:30 p.m.

Miércoles, 27 de marzo a las 7:30 p.m.

Jueves, 28 de marzo a las 7:30 p.m.

ATENCIÓN: Haga el favor de traer esta carta a la reunión que usted decida asistir ya que sin ella usted no podrá ser admitido. Además, a todos los invitados se los pagará $1.00 por concepto de gastos de ida y regreso de sus respectivos domicilios al Centro de Refugiados.

NO SE OLVIDE: Asista a una de estas reuniones, y traiga esta carta con usted.

Anticipándole nuestros agradecimientos,

RICHARD BRODY

Director del Proyecto

CUBAN REFUGEE EMERGENCY CENTER
600 Biscayne Boulevard
Miami 32, Florida

Miami, March 22, 1963

DEAR SIR:

This letter is to remind you that you have been selected as a member of a group of refugees who will be interviewed about their experiences in Cuba.

DON'T FORGET: Attend one of the following meetings in the Cuban Refugee Center, 600 Biscayne Boulevard, Miami.

Monday, March 25, at 7:30 p.m.
Tuesday, March 26, at 7:30 p.m.
Wednesday, March 27, at 7:30 p.m.
Thursday, March 28, at 7:30 p.m.

ATTENTION: Please bring the first letter (the 18th of March) to the meeting that you decide to attend because without it you cannot be admitted. Also, everyone will be paid $1.00 as reimbursement for round-trip expenses from his home to the Refugee Center.

We look forward to seeing you,
RICHARD BRODY
Project Director

The following note was added by the administration of the Refugee Center:

For your information and guidance we want to explain that this invitation to come to the Center has no bearing on your refugee status as it relates to employment, relocation, or economic aid.
The invitation deals with a university study about the refugees. We would appreciate your cooperation with Professor Brody.

CUBAN REFUGEE EMERGENCY CENTER
600 Biscayne Boulevard
Miami 32, Florida

Miami, el 22 de marzo de 1963

ESTIMADO SEÑOR:

Esta carta es para recordarle a Vd. que ha sido seleccionado para integrar un grupo de refugiados que serán entrevistados acerca de sus experiencias en Cuba.

NO SE OLVIDE: Asista a una de las siguientes reuniones en el Centro de Refugiados Cubanos, 600 Biscayne Boulevard, Miami.

Lunes, 25 de marzo a las 7:30 p.m.
Martes, 26 de marzo a las 7:30 p.m.
Miércoles, 27 de marzo a las 7:30 p.m.
Jueves, 28 de marzo a las 7:30 p.m.

ATENCIÓN: Haga el favor de traer la primera carta (el 18 de marzo) a la reunión que usted decida asistir ya que sin ella usted no podrá ser admitido. Además, a todos los invitados se los pagará $1.00 por concepto de gasto de ida y regreso de sus respectivos domicilios al Centro de Refugiados.

Anticipándole nuestros agradecimientos,

RICHARD BRODY
Director del Proyecto

The following note was added by the administration of the Refugee Center:

Para su información y gobierno deseamos explicarle que esta invitación a que acuda al Centro no tiene relación con su condición de refugiado en cuanto a empleo, relocalización o ayuda económica. Se trata de un estudio de una universidad en relación con los refugiados. Apreciaremos su cooperación al profesor Brody.

FINAL QUESTIONNAIRE—ENGLISH VERSION

Please read and answer all questions carefully and fully. Use all the time needed to answer the questions completely and legibly. If you need more space, use the reverse side of the pages.

Your help and cooperation are greatly appreciated.

1. How old are you? _____years.

2. What is your marital status?
   (Place a mark in front of the appropriate answer)
   _____not married
   _____married and wife is in the United States
   _____married and wife is not in the United States
   _____other (widower, divorcee, etc.)

3. Do you have any children less than 21 years old living in the United States? _____yes _____no
   If you have checked yes, how many live in the Miami area? (Give the number)_____
   How many live in other parts of the United States? (Give the number)_____

4. By what type of transportation did you come to the United States when you left Cuba?
   _____commercial airplane
   _____private boat
   _____other transportation (please specify what type)

5. When you lived in Cuba, where was your home?
   _____in Havana
   _____in some other large city
   (give name of city)_____
   _____in a small city or town (give name)_____
   _____in the countryside (give name of nearest city or town)_____

6. Do you still have close relatives living in Cuba?
   _____yes _____no
   If you have checked yes, how many still live there? (Give the number)_____
   What relation are they to you?_____

7. Please indicate the highest level of schooling you have achieved.

_____some grade school
_____finished grade school
_____some high school
_____finished high school
_____some university
_____finished university
_____professional degree (please indicate specialization)

_____

8. When you lived in Cuba, what was your occupation? That is, what did you actually do for a living? _____

9. Approximately how much money (in pesos) did you earn during 1958? _____pesos.

10. Approximately how much money (in pesos) did you earn during the last complete year you spent in Cuba? _____pesos.

11. Think back to 1958 when Batista was still in power. How did you feel toward the Batista government at that time? (Place a mark in front of the answer which comes closest to your feelings.)

_____I agreed with many of the Batista government's policies.

_____I agreed with some of the Batista government's policies.

_____I agreed with a few of its policies.

_____I agreed with none of its policies.

_____I hated the Batista tyranny.

12. Before Castro came to power, did you help him or help the revolutionary cause in any way? _____yes _____no
If you have checked yes, what was the nature of your help or contribution? (please check more than one category if appropriate)

_____fought with the rebels

_____worked in or with the underground

_____contributed money

_____contributed supplies or other services

_____other help or contribution (please specify the details) _____

13. When Castro first took over in 1959, which of the following best describes your feelings toward him at that time?

_____I thought he was the savior of Cuba.

_____I admired him a great deal.

_____I admired him some.

_____I admired him very little.

_____I did not admire him at all.

14. *During the first six months of 1959*, did Castro work toward accomplishing his announced aims and programs?

_____yes, he worked *very* hard toward accomplishing his announced aims and programs.

_____yes, he made some effort toward accomplishing his announced aims and programs.

_____yes, he made a little effort.

_____no, he made no effort at all.

15. How did you feel about the *revolutionary government* in general when it first came to power in 1959?

_____I felt very strongly that it was composed of honest and dedicated men.

_____I felt that it contained many honest and dedicated men.

_____I felt that it contained a few honest and dedicated men.

_____I felt that it contained no honest and dedicated men.

16. When the revolutionary government took over, did you at any time actively participate in its activities or lend your support in any other direct manner?

_____yes _____no

If you have checked yes, what was the nature of your participation or support? (check more than one category if appropriate)

_____I served officially in the government (specify position and dates of service). _____

_____I served in the armed forces or militia (specify rank and dates of service). _____

_____I served in some other revolutionary organization (specify type of organization and dates of participation). _____

_____Other form of participation or support (please specify the details). _____

17. On what date did you first begin to think about leaving Cuba?
    _____month _____year

18. Please tell us in detail why you began to think about leaving.
    Was there some incident (or incidents) in particular which
    awakened your uneasiness? If so, please tell us about this inci-
    dent (or incidents). _____

    _____

19. On what date did you actually decide to leave Cuba?
    _____month _____year

20. Please tell us in detail why you finally decided to leave. Was
    there some particular incident which was central to your deci-
    sion to leave? If so, please tell us about this incident. _____

    _____

21. On what date did you actually leave Cuba?
    _____month _____year

22. When you came to the United States did you already have close
    relatives here?   _____yes _____no
    If you have checked yes, how many were here? (Give the
    number)_____
    What relation were they to you? _____

23. When you came to the United States did you already have very
    close friends here?   _____yes _____no
    If you have checked yes, how many were here? (Give the
    number)_____

24. What aspect of your former life in Cuba do you miss most now
    that you are living in the United States? _____

    _____

25. What about the United States has disappointed you the most
    since you have been here? _____

26. What changes would have to be made in Cuba before you
    would want to return there to live? _____

27. Which Cubans do you feel have benefited most from the revo-
    lution? _____

28. Which Cubans do you feel have been hurt the most by the revo-
    lution? _____

29. What do you think the future holds in store for Cuba? That is,

given the situation which now prevails in Cuba, what important changes do you think might occur in the island in the next
two or three years? (*For example,* will there be *more* or *less*
food than there is now?) _____

30. What percentage of all the people living in Cuba do you think
would presently support a movement to overthrow the Castro
government?

_____less than 10% would support a movement to over-
throw the government.

_____between 10% and 30% would support such a move-
ment.

_____between 30% and 50% would support such a move-
ment.

_____between 50% and 70% would support such a move-
ment.

_____between 70% and 90% would support such a move-
ment.

_____over 90% would support a movement to overthrow
the government.

31. What are the one or two main reasons why most of the refugees left Cuba? _____

32. Which of the following best describes your feelings about
Castro *at the present time?*

_____I admire him some.

_____I admire him very little

_____I do not admire him at all.

_____I think he is one of the worst tyrants in the history of
Cuba.

33. How do you feel about the present government in Cuba?

_____The government contains some honest and dedicated
men.

_____The government contains a few honest and dedicated
men.

_____The government contains no honest and dedicated
men.

34. Who is the most hated man in Cuba today?
Please indicate by name_____

35. Please indicate which of these phrases *best* describes your
opinion about the following statements. (Put an × in front
of the phrase which best describes your feeling.)
During the last 50 years the United States has interfered too
much in the *political* affairs of Cuba.

_____strongly agree

_____agree

_____indifferent

_____disagree

_____strongly disagree

During the last 50 years the United States has interfered too
much in the *economic* affairs of Cuba.

_____strongly agree

_____agree

_____indifferent

_____disagree

_____strongly disagree

People in the United States have made every effort to welcome
and help the Cuban refugees.

_____strongly agree

_____agree

_____indifferent

_____disagree

_____strongly disagree

During the Batista days, many United States *tourists* behaved
badly when visiting Cuba.

_____strongly agree

_____agree

_____indifferent

_____disagree

_____strongly disagree

During the Batista days, many United States *businessmen* behaved badly when visiting Cuba.

_____strongly agree

_____agree

_____indifferent

_____disagree

_____strongly disagree

The government of the United States has always been in the right in its relations with Castro.

_____strongly agree

_____agree

_____indifferent

_____disagree

_____strongly disagree

A man can live a better and happier life in the United States than in any other country in the world.

_____strongly agree

_____agree

_____indifferent

_____disagree

_____strongly disagree

36. Have you been active in any Cuban refugee organizations since coming to the United States?

      _____yes _____no

If you have checked yes, please indicate the names of the organizations in which you have been active and the nature of your participation. _____

37. Please indicate your current employment. That is, how do you actually make a living at this time? _____

Thank you very much for your cooperation.

FINAL QUESTIONNAIRE—SPANISH VERSION

Por favor lea y conteste todas las preguntas completa y cuidadosamente. Use todo el tiempo que sea necesario para contestar las preguntas completa y legiblemente. Si le hace falta espacio, use el reverso de las hojas.

Agradecemos mucho su ayuda y cooperación.

1. ¿Cuántos años tiene Vd.? _____años.

2. ¿Cuál es su estado civil?
   (Ponga una X delante de la respuesta apropiada)
   _____soltero
   _____casado y con la esposa en los Estados Unidos
   _____casado y sin la esposa en los Estados Unidos
   _____otro (viudo, divorciado, etc.)

3. ¿Tiene Vd. hijos menores de 21 años viviendo en los Estados Unidos? _____sí _____no
   Si ha marcado "sí", ¿cuántos de ellos viven en Miami y sus vecindades? (Dé el número)_____
   ¿Cuántos viven en otras partes de los Estados Unidos? (Dé el número)_____

4. ¿En qué clase de transporte vino Vd. a los Estados Unidos cuando salió de Cuba?
   _____avión comercial
   _____barco privado
   _____otra forma de transporte (por favor especifique qué forma)_____

5. ¿Dónde vivía Vd. en Cuba?
   _____en La Habana
   _____en alguna otra ciudad grande (dé el nombre de la ciudad)_____
   _____en una ciudad pequeña o pueblo (dé el nombre)
   _____
   _____en el campo (dé el nombre de la ciudad o población más cercana)_____

6. ¿Quedan todavía algunos de sus parientes cercanos en Cuba?
   _____sí _____no

Si ha marcado "sí", ¿cuántos de ellos viven ahí todavía? (Dé el número)_____

¿Qué parentesco tienen con Vd.?_____

7. Por favor indique el nivel máximo de educación alcanzado por Vd.

_____algunos años de escuela primaria

_____terminé la escuela primaria

_____algunos años de escuela secundaria

_____terminé la escuela secundaria

_____algunas años de universidad

_____terminé la universidad

_____título profesional (por favor indique la especialización)_____

8. Cuando vivía Vd. en Cuba, ¿cuál era su ocupación? Es decir, ¿cómo se ganaba Vd. la vida?_____

9. ¿Aproximadamente cuánto dinero (en pesos) ganó Vd. durante el año de 1958? _____pesos.

10. ¿Más o menos cuánto dinero (en pesos) ganó Vd. durante los últimos doce meses que pasó en Cuba? _____pesos.

11. Recordando los días del año 1958 cuando Batista estaba todavía en el poder, ¿qué pensaba Vd. del gobierno batistiano en aquel tiempo? (Ponga una ✕ delante de la respuesta más aproximada a sus sentimientos.)

_____Estaba de acuerdo con *muchas* de las acciones del gobierno batistiano.

_____Estaba de acuerdo con *algunas* de las acciones del gobierno batistiano.

_____Estaba de acuerdo con *pocas* de sus acciones.

_____No aprobaba *ninguna* de sus acciones.

_____Odiaba la tiranía de Batista.

12. Antes de que Castro llegara al poder, ¿ayudó Vd. a él o a la causa revolucionaria de alguna manera?

_____sí _____no

Si ha marcado "sí", ¿en qué forma fué su ayuda o contribución? (Por favor marque más de una categoría si es el caso.)

_____luché con los rebeldes

_____trabajé en o cooperé con el movimiento clandestino

_____contribuí con dinero

_____contribuí con provisiones u otros servicios

_____otra ayuda o contribución (haga el favor de especificar los detalles). _____

13. Cuando Castro llegó al poder en 1959, ¿cuál de las siguientes frases describe mejor sus sentimientos hacia él en aquel momento?

_____Pensaba que era el salvador de Cuba.

_____Le admiraba muchísimo.

_____Le admiraba *un tanto*.

_____Le admiraba *muy poco*.

_____No le admiraba *nada*.

14. ¿Cree Vd. que *durante los seis primeros meses de 1959* Castro se empeñó en cumplir los programas y las metas que había anunciado?

_____sí, se empeñó *mucho* en cumplir los programas y las metas que había anunciado.

_____sí, hizo *algún* esfuerzo para conseguir los programas y las metas que había anunciado.

_____sí, hizo *poco* esfuerzo.

_____no, no hizo *ningún* esfuerzo.

15. ¿Qué pensaba Vd. en general del *gobierno revolucionario* cuando llegó al poder en 1959?

_____Creía firmemente que estaba compuesto por hombres honestos y dedicados.

_____Creía que en él habían *muchos* hombres honestos y dedicados.

_____Creía que en él habían *unos cuantos* hombres honestos y dedicados.

_____Creía que en él no había *ningún* hombre honesto y dedicado.

16. Una vez que el gobierno revolucionario tomó el poder, ¿participó Vd. alguna vez en él de una manera activa, o prestó Vd. su apoyo en alguna otra forma directa?

_____sí _____no

Si ha marcado "sí", ¿de qué manera participó o apoyó Vd.?
(marque más de una categoría si es el caso)

_____Serví oficialmente en el gobierno (especifique su cargo y las fechas de servicio). _____

_____Serví en las fuerzas armadas o en la milicia (especifique rango y fechas de servicio). _____

_____Serví en otra organización revolucionaria (especifique el tipo de organización y las fechas de participación). _____

_____Otra forma de participación o apoyo (por favor especifique los detalles). _____

17. ¿En qué fecha empezó Vd. a pensar en marcharse de Cuba?

_____mes _____año

18. Por favor, explique detalladamente por qué empezó Vd. a pensar en marcharse. ¿Hubo algún incidente (o incidentes) en particular que despertó su inquietud? Si es así, haga el favor de relatarnos este incidente (o incidentes). _____

19. ¿En qué fecha decidió Vd. irse de Cuba?

_____mes _____año

20. Por favor, díganos de una manera detallada por qué por fin se decidió a irse. ¿Hubo algún incidente en particular que influyera definitivamente en su decisión de partir? Si es así, haga el favor de relatarnos este incidente. _____

21. ¿En qué fecha salió Vd. de Cuba?

_____mes _____año

22. Cuando vino Vd. a los Estados Unidos, ¿ya tenía Vd. parientes cercanos aquí? _____sí _____no
Si ha marcado "sí", ¿cuántos estaban aquí? (Dé el número)

_____

¿Qué clase de parentesco tenían con Vd.? _____

23. Cuando vino a los Estados Unidos, ¿ya tenía Vd. amigos íntimos aquí? _____sí _____no
Si ha marcado "sí", ¿cuántos estaban aquí? (Dé el número)

_____

24. Ahora que está viviendo en los Estados Unidos, ¿cuál es el aspecto de su pasada vida en Cuba que más echa Vd. de menos? _____

25. ¿Qué es lo que más le ha desilusionado de los Estados Unidos desde que llegó aquí? _____

26. ¿Qué cambios tendrían que ocurrir en Cuba para que Vd. quisiera volver a vivir allí? _____

27. ¿Quiénes de los cubanos, cree Vd., que se han beneficiado más de la Revolución? _____

28. ¿Quiénes de los cubanos, cree Vd., que han sido dañados más por la Revolución? _____

29. ¿Qué cree Vd. que el futuro guarda para Cuba? Es decir, dada la situación que *hoy prevalece* en Cuba, ¿qué cambios importantes cree Vd. que pueden ocurrir en la isla en los dos o tres años próximos? (*Por ejemplo*, ¿habrá *más* o *menos* alimentos de los que existe hoy?). _____

30. ¿Qué porcentaje de la población ahora en Cuba cree Vd. apoyarían un movimiento para derrocar el gobierno de Castro?
    _____ menos del 10% apoyarían un movimiento para derrocar al gobierno.
    _____ entre 10 y 30 por ciento apoyarían tal movimiento.
    _____ entre 30 y 50 por ciento apoyarían tal movimiento.
    _____ entre 50 y 70 por ciento apoyarían tal movimiento.
    _____ entre 70 y 90 por ciento apoyarían tal movimiento.
    _____ más del 90 por ciento apoyarían un movimiento para derrocar al gobierno.

31. ¿Cuál es la razón o las dos razones más importantes por las que los refugiados han salido de Cuba? _____

32. ¿Cuál de las siguientes frases describe mejor sus sentimientos hacia Castro en la actualidad?
    _____ Le admiro *un poco*.
    _____ Le admiro *muy poco*.
    _____ No le admiro *nada*.
    _____ Creo que es uno de los peores tiranos en la historia de Cuba.

33. ¿Qué piensa Vd. del presente gobierno de Cuba?
    _____ En el gobierno hay *algunos* hombres honestos y dedicados.

_____En el gobierno hay *pocos* hombres honestos y dedicados.

_____En el gobierno no hay *ningún* hombre honesto y dedicado.

34. ¿Quién es el hombre más odiado en Cuba hoy día? Por favor indique el nombre _____

35. Haga el favor de indicar cuál de estas frases describe *mejor* su opinión acerca de las siguientes declaraciones. (Ponga una X delante de la frase que más se aproxima a su manera de sentir).

En los últimos 50 años los Estados Unidos han interferido demasiado en los asuntos *políticos* de Cuba.

_____completamente de acuerdo

_____de acuerdo

_____indiferente

_____en desacuerdo

_____completamente en desacuerdo

En los últimos 50 años los Estados Unidos han interferido demasiado en los asuntos *económicos* de Cuba.

_____completamente de acuerdo

_____de acuerdo

_____indiferente

_____en desacuerdo

_____completamente en desacuerdo

La gente en los Estados Unidos ha hecho todo lo posible para acoger y ayudar a los refugiados cubanos.

_____completamente de acuerdo

_____de acuerdo

_____indiferente

_____en desacuerdo

_____completamente en desacuerdo

Durante los días de Batista, muchos turistas americanos se portaban mal cuando visitaban Cuba.

_____completamente de acuerdo

_____de acuerdo

_____indiferente

_____en desacuerdo

_____completamente en desacuerdo

Durante los días de Batista muchos hombres de negocios americanos se portaban mal cuando visitaban Cuba.

_____completamente de acuerdo
_____de acuerdo
_____indiferente
_____en desacuerdo
_____completamente en desacuerdo

El gobierno de los Estados Unidos ha estado siempre en la
razón en sus relaciones con Castro.

_____completamente de acuerdo
_____de acuerdo
_____indiferente
_____en desacuerdo
_____completamente en desacuerdo

Un hombre puede vivir una vida mejor y más feliz en los
Estados Unidos que en cualquier otro país del mundo.

_____completamente de acuerdo
_____de acuerdo
_____indiferente
_____en desacuerdo
_____completamente en desacuerdo

36. ¿Ha participado activamente en alguna de las organizaciones
de los refugiados cubanos desde que vino a los Estados Unidos? _____sí _____no
Si ha marcado "sí", haga el favor de indicar los nombres de
las organizaciones en las cuales ha participado y también la
forma de su participación. _____

37. Haga el favor de indicar su empleo actual. Es decir, ¿cómo se
gana Vd. la vida en estos días? _____

Muchas gracias por su cooperación.

Appendix B

Table B.1

Comparative Age Distributions of Roster Sample, Respondents, Non-respondents, and Relocated Refugees

Age	Roster Sample[a] (N = 1096)	Respondents[b] (N = 209)	Non-respondents[c] (N = 179)	Relocated[d] (N = 327)
25 or younger	13%	4%	6%	18%
26 to 35	25	23	34	27
36 to 45	30.5	27.5	29	28
46 to 55	18	29	19	20
56 or older	13.5	16	12	7
No data	—	.5	—	—

[a] *Roster Sample:* A systematic sample by occupation taken from the list of the 59,682 employable Cubans who had registered with the Refugee Center by March 1963. This sample includes refugees who were relocated as well as those still in the Miami area.

[b] *Respondents:* The 209 heads of households who successfully filled out the questionnaire.

[c] *Non-respondents:* Heads of households who were in the original sample of 401 drawn, but who did not come to the Refugee Center and did not fill out the questionnaire. Of the original sample of 401 heads of households, 209 filled out the questionnaire correctly, and two came to the Center but were not able to complete the questionnaire. Of the 190 who did not come, demographic data were not available for 11; thus the final N for non-respondents is 179.

[d] *Relocated:* A percentage and numerical quota for each occupational group was established according to the proportional contribution of that occupation to the approximately 15,000 employable refugees who had been relocated by December 15, 1962. A sample of 327 was drawn according to these quotas by selecting every tenth name within each occupational group of relocated refugees until the established quota was filled for that group. The age, education, and date of departure (from Cuba) of each refugee selected was then taken from his record.

Table B.2

Comparative Educational Distributions of Roster Sample, Respondents, Non-respondents, and Relocated Refugees

Education	Roster sample (N = 1096)	Respondents (N = 209)	Non-respondents (N = 179)	Relocated (N = 327)
Some grammar school	45%	33%	45%	38.5%
Some secondary school	31	42	24	27
Some university	12.5	12	22	20
Professional degree	10.5	10	8	14
No data	1	3	1	.5

TABLE B.3

Comparative Occupational Distributions of Roster Sample,
Respondents, Non-respondents, and Relocated Refugees

Occupation	Roster sample (N = 1096)	Respondents (N = 209)	Non-respondents (N = 179)	Relocated (N = 327)
Professional and semiprofessional	23%[a]	16%	25%	31%[a]
Managerial and executive ..	13	22	17	6
Clerical and sales	31	25	24	33
Service	9	9	13	3
Skilled labor	14	8	7	11
Semiskilled and unskilled labor	7	11	11	14
Agricultural and fishing ...	3	8	3	1
No data	1	1	—	—

[a] The totals of these figures differ from 100 per cent because of rounding.

TABLE B.4

Comparative Date of Entry Distributions of Roster Sample,
Respondents, Non-respondents, and Relocated Refugees

Date of Entry into the United States	Roster sample (N = 1096)	Respondents[a] (N = 209)	Non-respondents (N = 179)	Relocated (N = 327)
During 1959	2%	7%[b]	3%	1%
During 1960	12	13	18	5.5
During 1961	31	30	43	31.5
During 1962	49	45	33	61.5
First three months of 1963..	6	4	2	—
No data	—	2	1	.5

[a] For respondents, date of departure from Cuba is reported rather than date of entry into the United States. Because over 80 per cent of the respondents flew directly from Havana to Miami, however, in most cases the two dates are the same.
[b] These figures total more than 100 per cent because of rounding.

CONSTRUCTION OF A GUTTMAN SCALE ON INITIAL
ATTITUDE TOWARD THE REVOLUTION

Final Order of Questions	Response Categories	Guttman Scoring
14. *During the first six months of 1959*, did Castro work toward accomplishing his announced aims and programs?	Yes, he worked *very hard*	1
	Yes, he made some effort	1
	Yes, he made a little effort	1
	No he made no effort at all	0
13. When Castro first took over in 1959, which of the following best describes your feelings toward him at that time?	Thought him the savior of Cuba	1
	I admired him a great deal	1
	I admired him some	1
	I admired him very little	0
	I did not admire him at all	0
11. Think back to 1958 when Batista was still in power. How did you feel toward the Batista government at that time?	I hated the Batista tyranny	1
	Agreed with no policies	1
	Agreed with few policies	1
	Agreed with some policies	0
	Agreed with many policies	0
15. How did you feel about the *revolutionary government* in general when it first came to power in 1959?	Honest and dedicated men (strong)	1
	Many honest and dedicated men	1
	A few honest and dedicated men	1
	No honest and dedicated men	0

Scale type   *N*

4 (most favorable)	23	
3	48	Coefficient of Reproducibility = .932
2	57	
1	47	Menzell Coefficient for Rows = .727
0 (least favorable)	34	
	———	Menzell Coefficient for Columns = .790
Total	209	

CONSTRUCTION OF A GUTTMAN SCALE OF CRITICISM
OF THE UNITED STATES
(Used to measure tendency to flatter)

Final Order of Questions	*Response Categories*	*Guttman Scoring*
35d. During the Batista days, many United States *tourists* behaved badly when visiting Cuba.	Strongly agree Agree Indifferent Disagree Strongly disagree	1 1 0 0 0
35e. During the Batista days, many United States *businessmen* behaved badly when visiting Cuba.	Strongly agree Agree Indifferent Disagree Strongly disagree	1 1 1 0 0
35f. The government of the United States has always been in the right in its relations with Castro.	Strongly disagree Disagree Indifferent Agree Strongly agree	1 1 1 0 0
35b. During the last 50 years, the United States has interfered too much in the *economic* affairs of Cuba.	Strongly agree Agree Indifferent Disagree Strongly disagree	1 1 1 0 0
35a. During the last 50 years, the United States has interfered too much in the *political* affairs of Cuba.	Strongly agree Agree Indifferent Disagree Strongly disagree	1 1 1 1 0

Scale type   *N*

5 (most critical)   18

4   15   Coefficient of Reproducibility = .929

3   39

2   53   Menzell Coefficient for Rows = .708

1   54

0 (least critical)   30   Menzell Coefficient for Columns = .779

Total   209

Notes

CHAPTER I

1. *Department of State Bulletin*, January 21, 1963, p. 89.
2. *Ibid.*
3. *Revolución*, December 31, 1962, p. 3. *Gusano* (worm) is the favorite epithet used by Castroites when referring to Cubans in exile (and "counterrevolutionaries" still on the island). For many months, *Revolución* published a daily column entitled *Gusanerías* ("worm doings"), which contained cartoons and short articles ridiculing the exile community in Miami.
4. Robert Dahl expresses this position as follows: "It would clear the air of a good deal of cant if instead of assuming that politics is a normal and natural concern of human beings, one were to make the contrary assumption that whatever lip service citizens may pay to conventional attitudes, politics is a remote, alien, and unrewarding activity. Instead of seeking to explain why citizens are not interested, concerned and active, the task is to explain why a few citizens *are*" (*Who Governs?* [New Haven, Conn., 1961], p. 279).
5. See Marcus Lee Hansen, *The Atlantic Migration, 1607–1860* (Cambridge, Mass., 1940); Oscar Handlin, *The Uprooted* (Boston, 1953); and Oscar Handlin, ed., *Immigration as a Factor in American History* (Englewood Cliffs, N.J., 1961).
6. For a useful survey of postwar refugee problems, see Joseph B. Schechtman, *The Refugee in the World* (New York, 1963). Some of the problems involved in the transfer of populations after the India-Pakistan division are considered in R. N. Saksena, *Refugees: A Study in Changing Attitudes* (New York, 1961). Arab resettlement is dealt with by Fred C. Brulius in "A Study of Arab Refugee Attitudes," *Middle East Journal*, IX, Spring 1955, 130–38.
7. On the Chinese, see Suzanne Labin, *The Anthill: The Human Condition in Communist China* (New York, 1960), a polemical but still useful account of interviews with refugees from the mainland. See also Edvard Hambro, *The Problem of Chinese Refugees in Hong Kong* (Leyden, 1955), and "Chinese Refugees in Hong Kong," *The Phylon Quarterly*, XVIII, April 1957, 69–81. On the Russian case, see Alex Inkeles and Raymond A. Bauer, *The Soviet Citizen* (Cambridge, Mass., 1959), and Raymond A. Bauer, "Some Trends in Sources of Alienation from the Soviet System," *Public Opinion Quarterly*, XIX, Fall 1955,

279–91. The circumstances surrounding the exile of the Soviet citizens studied by Inkeles and Bauer differ from those in the Cuban case. The majority of the Russians studied were displaced by the Second World War and later chose not to return to the Soviet Union; thus the Soviet case is not as clear an example of self-imposed political exile as is the Cuban. On Hungarian refugees, see Henry Gleitman and Joseph J. Greenbaum, "Hungarian Socio-Political Attitudes and Revolutionary Action," *Public Opinion Quarterly*, XXIV, Spring 1960, 62–76; Paul Zinner, "Revolution in Hungary: Reflections on the Vicissitudes of a Totalitarian System," *Journal of Politics*, XXI, February 1959, 3–36; Paul Kecskemeti, *The Unexpected Revolution* (Stanford, Calif., 1961); Lawrence E. Hinkle, Jr. *et al.*, "Hungarian Refugees: Life Experiences and Features Influencing Participation in the Revolution and Subsequent Flight," *American Journal of Psychiatry*, CXVI, July 1959, 16–19; and Eva Bene, "Anxiety and Emotional Impoverishment in Men under Stress," *British Journal of Medical Psychology*, XXXIV (1961), 281–89.

8. See, for example, Hadley Cantril, *The Pattern of Human Concerns* (New Brunswick, N.J., 1965), pp. 315–22.

9. For economic and social data on what has happened to Cuban refugees in Miami, see *The Cuban Immigration, 1959–1966, and Its Impact on Miami–Dade County, Florida* (Coral Gables, Fla., 1967). Published by the Center for Advanced International Studies, University of Miami.

10. In addition to the literature cited in note 7, see the following on the American case: Lorenzo Sabine, *Biographical Sketches of Loyalists of the American Revolution* (Boston, 1864), Vols. 1 and 2; C. H. Van Tyne, *The Loyalists in the American Revolution* (New York, 1902); A. G. Bradley, *Colonial Americans in Exile* (New York, 1932); and Edward Livingston Taylor, "Refugees to and from Canada and the Refugee Tract," *Ohio Archaeological and Historical Society Publications*, XIII (1903), 219–41. Persons who view the Cuban exodus as prima facie "proof" of the immorality of the Castro government would do well to recall that perhaps 100,000 loyalists were killed or forced into exile during the American Revolution (estimate from Van Tyne, p. vii).

11. The Cuban Refugee Emergency Center was established in December 1960, and opened early in 1961 when exiles from Cuba were already arriving in the United States at the rate of more than 1,000 weekly. Administratively, the Center is under the United States Department of Health, Education, and Welfare. In addition to providing a wide variety of social services, the Center, in cooperation with the United States Department of Labor, runs an extensive resettlement program designed to relocate Cubans in other areas of the United States. For more detail on the Center and its operations see John F. Thomas, "Cuban Refugee Program," *Welfare in Review*, I, 3 (Septem-

ber 1963). Published by the Department of Health, Education, and Welfare.

12. The records of the Center do not contain the names of *all* Cuban exiles, for it was not mandatory for them to register at the Center upon arriving in the United States. However, we do know something about what types of persons were less likely to register, and thus we know something about the types of bias that our dependence on the Center records introduced.

13. Reported in Inkeles and Bauer, *The Soviet Citizen,* I–III.

14. The payment for participation was kept at a token level not only because we could not afford to pay more, but also because we did not want to reward our respondents. Some respondents refused the dollar, saying that they would take no money for participating. The second letter and the attachment are reproduced in Appendix A.

15. Richard Brody, Thomas O'Leary and Franklin Maiguashca, then a graduate student at Stanford, participated in the data-gathering in Miami.

16. Evidently, even some of those who did not come to the Center felt a certain responsibility toward the project. We received 13 letters of apology and regret from exiles who said that they wanted to attend but were unable to do so. Some offered to correspond with us if they could help in any way.

CHAPTER II

1. This observation is based on informal interviews conducted by Richard Fagen in Cuba in the summer of 1966 and in Miami in the summer of 1963.

2. See Edwin M. Martin, "U.S. Outlines Policy Toward Cuban Refugees," *Department of State Bulletin,* June 24, 1963, pp. 983–90. Of all those who left Cuba in the wake of the Castro take-over, perhaps 85 per cent came to the United States. Others went to Puerto Rico, Mexico, Chile, other Latin American countries, and Spain. We have no data on exiles to countries other than the United States. On why it is impossible to say precisely how many Cuban exiles are in the United States or were here as of any given date, see *The Cuban Immigration, 1959–1966, and Its Impact on Miami–Dade County, Florida* (Coral Gables, Fla., 1967), pp. 3–6. Published by the Center for Advanced International Studies, University of Miami.

3. For a very rough estimate of the magnitude of this underrepresentation, we can note that Martin (see note 2) says that about 3,000 Cubans entered Miami during 1958 and the early months of 1959. The Refugee Center records show that 597 "employables" registered as having entered in 1958 or the first three months of 1959. If we assume that each "employable" represents three persons (himself and two de-

pendents), then the Center records account for 1,791 refugees, or approximately 60 per cent of the 3,000 mentioned by Martin.

4. We have used the 1953 census for these comparisons, rather than demographic information published in the mid-sixties. This "revolutionary" information reflects not only the impact of the extensive educational programs of the Castro government, but also the blurring of standard occupational categories owing to the influence of Marxist theory. In general, the comparisons make more sense when the social structure of pre-Castro Cuba is taken as the basis for comparison. The data in Tables 2.1, 2.2, and 2.3 were first reported in Richard R. Fagen and Richard A. Brody, "Cubans in Exile: A Demographic Analysis," *Social Problems*, XI, 4 (Spring 1964), 389–401.

5. The bias of the Refugee Center roster makes this estimate conservative. Because professionals and semiprofessionals are the occupational types least likely to register with the Refugee Center upon entering the United States, the overrepresentation is actually greater than that reported in Table 2.1.

6. Cuban census data are from Wyatt MacGaffey and Clifford R. Barnett, *Cuba* (New Haven, Conn., 1962), pp. 343–44. Data on the Cuban refugees cover the period from January 1959 to the end of September 1962. When doing analyses of the occupational composition of the refugee community, we shall consider only those exiles who arrived before this September cutoff date. After the missile crisis of October 1962, regular air service from Cuba to the United States ceased. Subsequently, the only refugees arriving in the United States were those few who escaped in small boats and those (mainly relatives of Bay of Pigs prisoners) who came on the ships that carried drugs and food (exchanged for the prisoners) to Havana. The use of this cutoff date explains the discrepancy between the total of 55,354 exiles used in this table and the total of 59,682 mentioned earlier in the text.

We were not able to obtain any data on the racial composition of the exile community. In 1966, however, members of the Research Institute for Cuba and the Caribbean at the University of Miami estimated that 2 per cent of the refugees were Negro and 3.5 per cent were part Negro. The 1953 Cuban census classified 12.4 per cent of the total population as Negro and 14.5 per cent as part Negro. See *The Cuban Immigration, 1959–1966*, p. 15.

7. Cuban census data for 1953 are from United Nations, *Compendium of Social Statistics: 1963* (New York, 1963), p. 314.

8. Census data are from United Nations, *Demographic Yearbook, 1960* (New York, 1960), pp. 184–85. Refugee percentages represent estimates from the roster sample (N = 1,075). The 1953 census did not present a breakdown by both occupation and age, so it is not possible to compare the Cuban workforce and the refugee workforce directly with respect to age.

9. Bruce M. Russett *et al.*, *World Handbook of Political and Social Indicators* (New Haven, Conn., 1964), p. 155.

10. José R. Alvarez Díaz *et al., Un Estudio Sobre Cuba* (Miami, Fla., 1963), p. 813.

11. Data on the home population are from Republic of Cuba, *Censos de Población, Viviendas y Electoral,* January 28, 1953, pp. 19–21.

12. The average age of refugees in the roster sample is 39.5, and the average age of refugees in the heads of households sample is 43.1. Using the t-test for the difference between two means, we find a t-value of 3.83, $p < .01$.

CHAPTER III

1. The question (26) was "What changes would have to be made in Cuba before you would want to return there to live?" The overwhelming majority of responses were expressed in terms of the downfall of Castro, the end of Communism, the end of tyranny, or the establishment of a democratic government. Only four respondents wrote specifically about a return to pre-Castro days, thus imputing desirable political qualities to the Batista period.

2. See question 32 in Appendix A, p. 136.

3. The question (33) was "How do you feel about the present government in Cuba?" The response categories and the percentages ($N = 189$) checking them were: The government contains some honest and dedicated men (1 per cent), The government contains a few honest and dedicated men (8 per cent), The government contains no honest and dedicated men (91 per cent).

4. The question (34) was "Who is the most hated man in Cuba today?" Of the 8 per cent not mentioning Castro by name, about half mentioned some other individual and about half mentioned some group or agency.

5. The question (29) was "What do you think the future holds in store for Cuba? That is, given the situation that now prevails in Cuba, what important changes do you think might occur on the island in the next two or three years?" Other data indicate that over time the number of exiles expecting the end of the Castro regime has diminished, eroded by their continued residence in the United States and by events on the island. In a special survey conducted in the exile community in 1966, when asked if there were Cubans working on the island to overthrow Castro and if these anti-Castro efforts would be successful, about 38 per cent of all respondents answered both questions affirmatively. For a discussion of these data and some qualitative impressions of the increasing pessimism among the refugees with regard to probable developments in Cuba, see *The Cuban Immigration, 1959–1966, and Its Impact on Miami–Dade County, Florida* (Coral Gables, Fla., 1967), pp. 119–23. Published by the Center for Advanced International Studies, University of Miami. The sample base of this survey is not given in the cited report.

6. The classic statement of this interpretation can be found in the white paper issued by the State Department in April 1961, just prior to the Bay of Pigs invasion. The first section of the white paper is titled "The Betrayal of the Cuban Revolution." In a typical passage, the assertion is made that "The history of the Castro Revolution ... has been the history of the disillusion, persecution, imprisonment, exile, and execution of men and women who supported Dr. Castro—in many cases fought by his side—and thereafter doomed themselves by trying to make his regime live up to his own promises" (reprinted in Robert F. Smith, *What Happened in Cuba? A Documentary History* [New York, 1963], p. 314).

7. This is a Guttman scale with a coefficient of reproducibility of .932, a Menzell coefficient for rows of .727, and a Menzell coefficient for columns of .790. Scale construction details are in Appendix B.

8. We consider the question on attitudes toward the Batista government to be an integral part of the dimension "initial attitude toward the revolution." In our sample, anti-Batista sentiments correlate so closely with pro-Castro feelings (in 1959) that no analytical advantage is obtained by treating the two subdimensions separately.

9. For comparison, the best available data for the home population indicate that in the spring of 1960 approximately 86 per cent of all adult Cubans supported the revolutionary government. Of these, one-half were classified as "moderate" supporters and one-half as "fervent" supporters. Because these estimates were based on a sample of 500 in Havana and 500 in other urban and semi-urban centers, they are probably somewhat conservative when applied to all adults in Cuba. The rural population was, if anything, even more strongly in favor of the revolution than the urban and semi-urban population. See Lloyd A. Free, *Attitudes of the Cuban People Toward the Castro Regime* (Princeton, N.J., 1960), p. 3.

10. For a discussion of the problem of bias resulting from possible exile tendencies to "flatter" their hosts, see the methodological note at the end of this chapter.

11. Free, p. 5. Similarly, Inkeles and Bauer found that among Russian emigrés, younger people were less likely than their elders to have always opposed the Communist regime (see Raymond A. Bauer, "Some Trends in Sources of Alienation from the Soviet System," *Public Opinion Quarterly*, XIX, Fall 1955, 287). In the case of Russian exiles, the differences between generations reflect, in part, differences between those who "grew up" under Communism and those who did not. A similar distinction can be made in the Cuban case only insofar as younger refugees became "politically aware" during the most romantic and dramatic phase of the rebellion against Batista. Maurice Zeitlin has discussed the impact of historical or prerevolutionary socializing experiences on different generations of the Cuban working class. In 1962 he found that among all Cuban workers, those from 28 to 35 years of age

were most favorable toward the revolutionary regime. The pattern of support found by Zeitlin, however, does not follow a simple progression from most support among the youngest to least support among the oldest. See Maurice Zeitlin, "Political Generations in the Cuban Working Class," *American Journal of Sociology*, LXXI, 5 (March 1966), 493–508, and *Revolutionary Politics and the Cuban Working Class* (Princeton, N.J., 1967).

12. This can be viewed as a special case of the frequently documented relationship between youth and "liberalism," or—conversely—between age and "conservatism." See, for example, Raymond A. Bauer *et al.*, *American Business and Public Policy* (New York, 1963), p. 86; Angus Campbell *et al.*, *The American Voter* (New York, 1960), p. 210; and Robert Lane, *Political Life* (Glencoe, Ill., 1959), pp. 258ff.

13. Free, p. 5. Because of the large size of Free's sample, these are statistically significant differences.

14. *Ibid.* All differences are statistically significant.

15. In the refugee community, prerevolutionary income does not seem to be a good indicator of initial attitude toward the revolution. There is, for instance, no consistent relationship between income in 1958 and attitude toward the revolution in 1959. Those in the highest income group (those earning more than $8,000) did tend to be slightly less favorable toward the revolution than those in the lower two groups; however, the upper income group contained older refugees in numbers sufficiently disproportionate to explain this tendency.

CHAPTER IV

1. See V. O. Key, Jr., *Public Opinion and American Democracy* (New York, 1961), Chapters 9 and 18; Robert E. Lane, *Political Life* (Glencoe, Ill., 1959), *passim*; Lester W. Milbrath, *Political Participation* (Chicago, 1965), particularly Chapter One; and Stanley Kelley, Jr., Richard E. Ayres, and William G. Bowen, "Registration and Voting: Putting First Things First," *American Political Science Review*, LXI, 2 (June 1967), 359–79.

2. On the anatomy of anti-Batista movements, see Jules Dubois, *Fidel Castro: Rebel—Liberator or Dictator?* (Indianapolis, 1959), and Robert Taber, *M-26: The Biography of a Revolution* (New York, 1961). Although the authors represent quite different political positions, they are in substantial agreement on the causes and extent of anti-Batista activity in Cuba in the late 1950's.

3. For instance, Taber, no friend of the Cuban upper classes, says that during 1957 "underground stations were established in each city throughout the island, and slowly, almost reluctantly, the business and prosperous professional classes began to turn their considerable means and influence into revolutionary channels" (Taber, p. 88).

4. Because of lack of data, we are forced to use our scale of initial attitude toward the revolution in 1959 as the measure of attitudes toward both Batista and the rebels in 1957 and 1958. We assume that our scale of initial attitude toward the revolution in 1959 would correlate very highly with a scale of these earlier attitudes if such a scale were available. This assumption is supported by the fact that a question concerning attitude toward Batista in 1958 "when Batista was still in power" formed part of the scale of initial attitude toward the revolution, along with three other questions on Castro and his government in 1959.

5. As was the case with our retrospective questions about initial attitudes toward the revolution, the retrospective questions about participation in rebel activity were not easy for a person in exile in Miami to answer in the affirmative. Nevertheless, as indicated in Table 4.1, one of every three refugees admitted having engaged in some form of pro-rebel activity. Even if this ratio of one participant to two nonparticipants is an underestimation of the true extent of refugee activity, it still indicates a rather high level of active support, given what we know about levels of political participation in other countries and under other conditions.

6. Strong support for the hypothesis is found in our otherwise unused data on 18 members of two exile organizations—the *Movimiento Unidad Revolucionaria* and the pilots in exile—most of whom also belonged to the *Movimiento de Recuperación Revolucionaria* (see Chapter I). Of these 18 refugees, 17 were clearly active in political organizations in Miami. (We did not consider the pilots in exile a political organization, although the association did have strong political overtones; we therefore checked to see whether or not they belonged to other organizations that were unambiguously political.) Of the 17 who belonged to exile political organizations, all but two had participated in the struggle against Batista.

CHAPTER V

Much of the data used in the first part of this chapter was first published in somewhat different form in Richard R. Fagen and Richard A. Brody, "Cubans in Exile: A Demographic Analysis," *Social Problems,* XI (Spring 1964), 389–401. All data reported in Figures 5.1 through 5.4 and Table 5.1 are either from the roster of employable refugees or from the roster sample.

1. We are assuming that for each employable refugee who registered at the Refugee Center there were, on the average, three dependents or non-registrants.

2. We examined twenty books and many articles in our search for at least a partial "theory" of emigration. Only two writers offer discussions

detailed enough to warrant mention here. Theodore Draper, in *Castro's Revolution* (New York, 1962), gives a brief explication of the refugee flow and concludes that "The emigration was top-heavy with businessmen, professionals, and intellectuals, but skilled and semiskilled workers were conspicuous in the later stages of the outpouring. Nevertheless, the Cuban exiles were hardly representative of Cuban society as a whole" (p. 61). Our data support this broad-gauge analysis. Second, Edwin M. Martin, in "U.S. Outlines Policy Toward Cuban Refugees," *Department of State Bulletin*, June 24, 1963, pp. 983–90, suggests that the emigration "can be divided ... into four reasonably distinct waves": (1) supporters of the Batista regime and the old military in the early part of 1959, (2) upper economic and social strata in the latter part of 1959 and the first ten months of 1960, (3) upper and middle social and economic classes, professionals, and businessmen from the end of 1960 to the middle of 1961, (4) office and factory workers, small merchants, and some fishermen and peasants from the middle of 1961 to October 1962. Although some elements of this "wave" model (such as the early flight of the military) are supported by our data, it seems to us to impose a too precise and not particularly accurate order on the emigration.

3. All of the differences reported in Table 5.1 are significant at the $p < .01$ level (see Fagen and Brody, pp. 398–99). Approximately 80 per cent of all the employable refugees registered with the Center in Miami had entered the United States after the beginning of 1961. Thus, the data reported in Table 5.1 are based on a large majority of the employable refugee population, although they cover only two of the four years under consideration. During 1959 and 1960, in part perhaps because we were dealing with rather small subsamples, we found no systematic trend in either the average age or the average educational level of employable refugees.

4. See Fagen and Brody, pp. 398–400.

5. We tested the fourth assumption by constructing an index of the "period of indecision," or the length of time taken by the refugees to make the decision to leave. Each respondent was asked to indicate the month in which he first began to think about leaving Cuba and the month in which he finally decided to leave. The calendar quarters from the beginning of 1959 to the end of 1962 were numbered from one to 16, and the number of the quarter in which the respondent first began to think about leaving was subtracted from the number of the quarter in which he decided to leave. In our sample, the index runs from zero (less than one quarter) to eight (24–26 months). When the index is run against the dichotomy "participated in the struggle against Batista"— "did not participate," no difference in the mean period of time taken to make the decision is found between the two groups. However, when we dichotomize the respondents with regard to their initial attitudes toward the revolution, we find that the fourth assumption is supported

by the data. That is, those who were initially less favorable toward the revolution took on the average less time to come to the decision to leave than those who were initially more favorable. This relationship is illustrated in the table below, in which the period of indecision is dichotomized at the overall mean (i.e., between two and three quarters).

Length of Decision Period by Initial Attitude
Toward the Revolution

	Initial Attitude Toward the Revolution	
Period of Indecision	Less Favorable (N = 115)	More Favorable (N = 59)
Less than three quarters..........	64%	49%
Three or more quarters	36	51
Chi-square = 3.73	$p < .10$	

6. In this and all similar analyses we have used the date on which the respondent said he irrevocably decided to leave the island instead of the date on which he left. Because of the difficulty of securing permission to leave Cuba and obtaining transportation to the United States after the break in diplomatic relations, the two dates often differ by many months. Although the date of decision is less precise and more subject to error on the part of the respondent than the date of departure, we gain two compensatory advantages by using it. First, the date of decision is conceptually more defensible than the date of departure, even with errors of recall, because it is the most direct estimate of the time of disaffection—at the moment, our pivotal dependent variable. Second, the dates of decision are more evenly distributed over the four years under consideration than are the dates of departure, enhancing the possibilities for analysis. In any event, the issue is not critical, because the relationships reported in Tables 5.2 and 5.3 are only slightly weakened if dates of departure are substituted for dates of decision. In Figures 5.1 through 5.4 and Table 5.1, presented earlier in this chapter, we would have used dates of decision instead of dates of entry into the United States had such data been available from the roster of the Refugee Center.

CHAPTER VI

1. Only those who were actually imprisoned are included in this category. Many others were arrested or detained for a few hours but were later released; they are classified here as harassed or persecuted (see categories 3 and 4).

We have no way of directly checking the validity of these and other responses to our questions about reasons for leaving. Because we had to depend on the respondent's own characterization of how the revolution affected him, we ran the risk of compiling a catalog of social and political horrors that bore little resemblance to the actual situation in Cuba at the time. However, as the quotations included in this chapter make clear, in the main the refugees cited incidents that do not at all strain an outside observer's credibility. There *were* arrests, and there *was* harassment, confiscation, indoctrination, loss of jobs, and curtailment of civil liberties under Castro; and these are precisely the kinds of experiences respondents cited. Whether one believes that all or some of these actions were justified and/or necessary is, for the moment, not relevant. They occurred, and the exiles were affected and alienated by them. In reading all 209 completed questionnaires, we did not find a single response that seemed a deliberate falsification intended to convince the investigators that the Castro government was composed of murderous beasts. We found no tales of the rape of young girls, no stories of men tortured to death, and no vignettes in which guards forced prisoners to dig their own graves before executing them. If the refugees in our sample believed that such things happened in Cuba, they did not volunteer the information in response to any of our questions. Thus, the most likely form of error in the responses given us is not deliberate falsification of the above sort, but rather the type of error that occurs in almost all surveys in which "why" questions are asked. For example, a respondent who cites the lack of civil rights in Cuba as a primary reason for leaving may well be masking (intentionally or unintentionally) economic motivations resulting from the confiscation of his business or lands. However, unlike many other studies utilizing "why" questions, in which the prevailing social and cultural environments make certain responses difficult to give—for example, "Why did you move out of the neighborhood?" (asked when Negro families are moving in)—in our study there were few if any obviously "acceptable" as opposed to "less acceptable" responses. Thus, we are not greatly concerned with the effects of this type of response error. Again, as anyone familiar with the revolution would attest, there is high apparent validity to the content and distribution of the responses we received.

2. For a brief discussion of the Committees, see Richard R. Fagen, "Mass Mobilization in Cuba: The Symbolism of Struggle," *Journal of International Affairs*, XX, 2 (1966), 260–61. For a more detailed discussion, see Fagen's forthcoming study of the transformation of political culture in Cuba to be published by Stanford University Press.

3. There is obviously some overlap between categories 3 and 4. We attempted to minimize ambiguity by requiring that a refugee classified as persecuted or harassed for failure to integrate must have said so specifically. He must have said that he was asked or expected to do X, Y, or Z and refused to do so with consequences A, B, or C. Thus, respondents who said—as some of those quoted in this chapter did—that

they were under surveillance because they did not "cooperate" with their co-workers or neighbors were *not* classified as persecuted or harassed because of their failure to integrate. Almost by definition, all the refugees in the survey sample were nonintegrated when they left Cuba, and almost all had been persecuted to some extent. For purposes of category 4, we were interested only in isolating that subgroup whose members specifically identified themselves as having suffered certain reprisals as a direct result of failure to participate in revolutionary activities.

4. Quoted in Lee Lockwood, *Castro's Cuba, Cuba's Fidel* (New York, 1967), p. 205.

5. Of those who had lost income, about 44 per cent cited figures indicating that during their final 12 months in Cuba their incomes were less than one-half of what they had been before Castro came to power. As one might expect, income loss and gain are related to initial attitude toward the revolution. Of all those who gained income under Castro, 53 per cent had favorable initial attitudes toward the revolutionary government. Among those who lost income, only 29 per cent had favorable initial attitudes (the difference is significant at the .02 level). One should not infer from this relationship, however, that punitive economic measures were directed against those who were initially less favorable toward the revolution. As we have previously noted, the less favorable group was so located in the socioeconomic structure of prerevolutionary Cuba that in the natural course of events its members were hit hardest by reforms. Thus, socioeconomic position in prerevolutionary Cuba aids in predicting both initial attitudes toward the revolution and the probability of loss of income. No direct economic retaliation against those who were initially less favorable toward the revolution need be assumed.

6. Similar findings with regard to the relative unimportance of economic motivations among Hungarian refugees are reported in Lawrence E. Hinkle *et al.*, "Hungarian Refugees: Life Experiences and Features Influencing Participation in the Revolution and Subsequent Flight," *American Journal of Psychiatry*, CXVI, July 1959, 16-19.

7. This is similar to what Gleitman and Greenbaum, in their study of Hungarian refugees, characterize as disaffection resulting from "the disruption of well-established social and cultural patterns through the attempted imposition of an alien system" (see Henry Gleitman and Joseph J. Greenbaum, "Hungarian Sociopolitical Attitudes and Revolutionary Action," *Public Opinion Quarterly*, XXIV, Spring 1960, 65).

8. See Table 6.1. We decided against combining secondary and primary responses in constructing Table 6.2. The total per cent of multiple responses is always, of course, more than 100. For comparisons of the relative importance of experiences, the inflated percentages that make up this total are, in our view, misleading. Similarly, we have not presented a separate analysis of second responses to the two questions. The pattern of second responses tends to follow the pattern of first responses, and what differences there are do not warrant inclusion here.

9. Our definition is very similar to that used by Bauer in his study of Soviet emigrés. He analyzes "ideological sources of alienation," opposing these by inference to more concrete sources such as imprisonment and exposure to Western influence. Bauer writes of his coding procedure: "The term 'ideological' was very broadly defined and included such things as 'absence of personal freedom' which are 'ideological' only under the broadest possible definition of the term" (see Raymond A. Bauer, "Some Trends in Sources of Alienation from the Soviet System," *Public Opinion Quarterly*, XIX, Fall 1955, 287).

10. Among other variables that are *not* related to type of experience cited are the dichotomy "Lost income under the revolution—gained income or income unchanged" and the dichotomy "Earned less than $4,000 in 1958—earned more than $4,000 in 1958."

11. On the pragmatic-ideological dichotomy, the 71 respondents with some secondary education split 36–35. The 36 respondents with some university education split 18–18.

12. As might be expected, participation in the struggle against Batista is positively related to the citation of ideological experiences. With our small sample, however, it is not possible to demonstrate that participation exercises an independent influence over the type of experience cited when the relationship is controlled for education and initial attitude toward the revolution.

CHAPTER VII

1. Morton Grodzins describes the process as follows: "When sorrows overbalance joys, when the cause of sorrow can be traced to an existing allegiance, and when an alternative is available, the stage is set for a shift in loyalty" (*The Loyal and the Disloyal* [Chicago, 1956], p. 197). Grodzins' concern is with *shifts in loyalty* as opposed to our focus on disaffection leading to exile (without necessarily or usually involving a new allegiance). Nevertheless, the key elements in the two processes are similar.

2. Quoted in Lee Lockwood, *Castro's Cuba, Cuba's Fidel* (New York, 1967), p. 250.

3. During a visit to Cuba in the summer of 1966, Richard Fagen tried to talk to as many Cubans as possible to find out why they had opted for continued participation in the revolution rather than exile. This "research" was completely unsystematic, and useful primarily in disabusing the author of the common American image of Cuba as an island seething with discontent.

4. Reported in an Associated Press dispatch from Varadero, Cuba (*Palo Alto Times*, April 5, 1967, p. 28) and adjusted upward to take into account the larger estimates in the *New York Times* (November 7, 1965, p. 1) made at the time the airlift agreement was signed and repeated frequently since then.

5. When most of the unwilling non-exiles are finally out of Cuba, perhaps 500,000, or 7.1 per cent, of a total (1960) population of 7,000,000 will have left since the beginning of 1959. This projection is based on the following estimates: Approximately 215,000 Cubans entered the United States between the end of 1959 and the early months of 1963. Perhaps 35,000 left Cuba and went to countries other than the United States during the same period. Approximately 250,000 have left since the beginning of 1963 or will leave in the future. The vast majority of the latter group have come or will come on the airlift that began in December 1965. Under the agreement between the United States and Cuba establishing the airlift, relatives of those already in the United States have priority in leaving Cuba. (See the *New York Times*, November 7, 1965, pp. 1 and 37. For a translation of the agreement, see Appendix A of *The Cuban Immigration, 1959–1966, and Its Impact on Miami–Dade County, Florida* [Coral Gables, Fla., 1967].)

Although the two events received a great deal of public attention, only about 3,000 Cubans came to the United States in the wake of the release of the Bay of Pigs prisoners (mainly aged, infirm, and relatives of the prisoners), and only about 3,000 more came in the open (legal) traffic of boats during October and November of 1965, when the airlift agreement was being negotiated. Of course, exiles have been arriving in Florida in small boats throughout the 1960's, having left Cuba without the permission of the Cuban authorities. It was reported by the Cuban Refugee Emergency Center in December 1966 that 9,458 persons had arrived in 1,017 boats since June 1961 (*ibid.*, p. 11).

6. "Economic Insecurity and the Political Attitudes of Cuban Workers," *American Sociological Review*, XXXI, February 1966, 35–51. See also Maurice Zeitlin, *Revolutionary Politics and the Cuban Working Class* (Princeton, N.J., 1967).

7. Zeitlin, "Economic Insecurity," p. 41.

8. Lloyd A. Free, *Attitudes of the Cuban People Toward the Castro Regime* (Princeton, N.J., 1960). Free classified 86 per cent of his respondents (urban and semi-urban sample only) as supporters of the regime.

9. A useful qualitative description of the attitudes and life-styles of some "disgustados" (those who are disgusted with the revolution but do not opt for exile) is to be found in Jose Yglesias, *In the Fist of the Revolution* (New York, 1968), especially Chapters 4–7. Edmundo Desnoes, in *Inconsolable Memories* (New York, 1967), draws an extremely sensitive portrait of a middle-class Cuban intellectual's ambivalence toward the revolution.

10. Seymour Martin Lipset, *Political Man* (Garden City, N.Y., 1960), p. 77.

11. For a recent evaluation see James Nelson Goodsell, "Castro Support Seems Rooted Among Youth," *Christian Science Monitor*, August 22, 1967, p. 10. Goodsell's evaluation concurs substantially with ob-

servations made by Richard Fagen during a visit to Cuba approximately one year earlier.

12. For more detailed comments and a bibliography see Richard R. Fagen, "Charismatic Authority and the Leadership of Fidel Castro," *Western Political Quarterly*, XVIII, June 1965, 275–84.

13. The best available description of Castro at work among the Cuban masses is to be found in Lockwood, *Castro's Cuba, Cuba's Fidel*.

14. See Eric Hoffer, *The Ordeal of Change* (New York, 1964).

15. In addition to being the years during which changes were most rapid and profound, 1961 and 1962 were also the years of greatest political arbitrariness and the most acute individual insecurity. Some of this was a consequence of the struggle between the "new" and the "old" Cuban Communists, a struggle that broke into the open only in the spring of 1962, although it had been simmering since some time in 1961. In his famous speech of March 26, 1962, Castro said that "a veritable chaos, a veritable anarchy" was being introduced into the nation because of the arbitrariness and favoritism of certain political cadres. (See *El Mundo*, March 27, 1962, pp. 5–9 for the entire speech. See also Boris Goldenberg, *The Cuban Revolution and Latin America* [New York, 1965], pp. 260–68 for a brief description of the political crisis and its antecedents.) The point to be noted is that the period of the most profound social and economic change coincided with the rule (primarily at lower levels) of many despotic and self-serving political cadres. It was not a situation conducive to winning ambivalent citizens over to the side of the revolution.

16. From a speech made by Castro at the time of the exodus from Camarioca (*Granma*, November 8, 1965, p. 5).

17. Luis Suardíaz, "Testigo de Cargo," *Cuban Poetry, 1959–1966* (Havana, 1967). This is a slightly modified version of the translation by Claudia Beck.

18. *Revolución*, September 30, 1961, p. 14.

19. More recently, Castro has been increasingly harsh toward those who have declared their intention of leaving but are still on the island. For instance, his speech on the seventh anniversary of the victory over the invading force at the Bay of Pigs (April 19, 1968) contained the following passage (*Granma*, Weekly Edition in English, April 28, 1968, p. 3):

We must say that, at the present moment, everybody is working, [including the] loafers—those who have made applications to leave the country. Prior to the revolutionary offensive [a mass participation campaign launched in March of 1968] it was a "*gusanos*' holiday"; the people were engaged in great tasks, and the *gusanos* were stabbing the people in the back, using every weapon and means available, living a life of ease.... Their attitude was: "Situation normal. Now let's get busy and take the first places in the queue; start the rumors and lower morale!"

But the Revolution has launched an offensive in every sphere of work.... The *gusanos* are no longer on holiday, waiting three years, living at the expense of others, yearning for the day when they will enter the Yankee "paradise." Not any more. The way to Miami now runs through the countryside, through the canefields, through work.

20. Even though it is not about Cuba, perhaps no recent book is as useful for putting the costs of the Cuban case into historical perspective as Barrington Moore, Jr., *Social Origins of Dictatorship and Democracy* (Boston, 1967), particularly Part Three.

Index

Moslem refugees, 5–6
Movimiento de Recuperación Revolucionaria, 150
Movimiento Unidad Revolucionaria, 14, 150

Occupations, Cuban work force and refugees, *see under* Demography
O'Leary, Thomas, 145
Organization of American States, 113

Partido Socialista Popular, 89, 111
Playa Girón, 67. *See also* Bay of Pigs
Political exile, varieties of, 3–9, 101–3
Political participation, *see* Attitudes; Batista, Fulgencio; Castro, Fidel; Demography
Puerto Rican refugees, 4, 4–5n

Refugee Center, *see* Cuban Refugee Emergency Center
Refugees: demography of, 19–24; initial support for revolution, 35–44; attitudes toward Batista, 49–50, 52–53; participation in anti-Batista activities, 49–56, 61; participation in anti-Castro activities, 55–61; number arriving in U.S., 62–64; changes in occupational composition of, 64–68; changes in age composition of, 68–69; changes in educational composition of, 69; time of decision to leave, 70–73; experiences affecting decision to leave, 78–88, 90–95; educational level and decision to leave, 95–98
Research design, 9–15, 24–28, 121–40. *See also* Methodology
Revolución, 2, 143, 157
Revolution, *see* Castro, Fidel; Cuban revolution

Russett, Bruce M., 146
Russian refugees, 6

Sabine, Lorenzo, 144
Saksena, R. N., 143
Sampling, 11–14. *See also* Methodology; Research design
Schechtman, Joseph B., 143
Senior, Clarence, 4n
Sierra Maestra, 34, 44, 49n, 75
Siquitrillados, 86, 86n
Smith, Robert F., 148
Steiner, Gary, 8n
Suardíaz, Luis, 157

Taber, Robert, 149
Taylor, Edward Livingston, 144
Thomas, John F., 144
Trujillo Molina, Rafael, 99–100
Twenty-Sixth of July Movement, 100

United States, 3ff, 18, 29, 33, 45–47, 48, 56–57, 82, 84, 117; and Bay of Pigs invasion, 1–2; immigration movements to, 4–9; refugee perceptions of, 45–47; and Cuban immigration, 62–64, 100–104 *passim*, 113
Urban Reform Law, 66
Urrutia, Manuel, 68
Uruguay, 5n

Van Tyne, C. H., 144
Varadero, 75; airlift, 104, 116

Wittke, Carl F., 5n

Yglesias, José, 156

Zeitlin, Maurice, 108, 148–49, 156
Zinner, Paul, 144